* * *

Enlightened Indigo Child
A Personal Guide to Flourishing with a Sixth Sense

* * *

Copyright © 2012 by Idelle Brand and Diandra Brand

All rights reserved. No part of this book may be reproduced by any mechanical, photographic, or electronic process, or in the form of a phonographic recording; nor may it be stored in a retrieval system, transmitted or otherwise be copied for public or private use-other than for "fair use" as brief quotations embodied in articles and reviews without prior written permission of the publisher.

Disclaimer

The authors of this book do not dispense medical advice or prescribe the use of any technique as a form of treatment for physical or medical problems. Please consult with a physician directly. The intent of the authors is only to offer information of a general nature to help you in your quest for emotional and spiritual well being. In the event that you use any of the information in this book for yourself, which is your constitutional right, the authors and the publisher assume no responsibility for your action.

Enlightened Indigo Child
A Personal Guide to Flourishing with a Sixth Sense

Idelle Brand
and
Diandra Brand

Acknowledgement

A big thank you to Source.
Nothing more.
Nothing less.
You have always provided.

There is a river flowing now very fast. It is so great and swift that there are those who will be afraid. They will try to hold onto the shore. They will feel that they are being torn apart, and they will suffer greatly.

Know the river has it's destination. The elders say we must let go of the shore. Push off into the middle of the river, keep our eyes open, and our heads above the water. See who is in there with you and celebrate. At this time in history, we are to take nothing personally.

Least of all, ourselves. For the moment that we do, our spiritual growth and journey comes to a halt.

The time of the lone wolf is over. Gather yourselves!

Banish the word struggle from your attitude and your vocabulary. All that we do now must be done in a sacred manner and in celebration.

We are the ones we have been waiting for.

---The Elders Oraibi, Arizona Hopi Nation

✽ ✽ ✽

Come to the edge.
We can't. We're afraid.
Come to the edge.
We can't. We will fall.
Come to the edge.

And they came.
And he pushed them.
And they flew.

---Guillaume Apollinaire, French Poet

* * *

CONTENTS

Introduction..1

Chapter 1   In the Beginning: Mom's Story....................7

Chapter 2   In the Beginning: Diandra's Story...............23

Chapter 3   Am I an Indigo?...37

Chapter 4   Indigos Are People Too!..............................47

Chapter 5   Indigos Who Are Intuitive 53

Chapter 6   Our Daily Environment...............................75

Chapter 7   Parents: Problems and Solutions...............121

Chapter 8   Own Your Power.......................................141

Chapter 9   Where Do We Go From Here?..................169

* * *
Introduction

Books about Indigo Children are few and far between. When you do find them, they are written from the perspective of the professional looking in, evaluating and analyzing. The tone of these authors is of managing the children as if they were animals in the zoo, oddities in the circus, or very unwell children with emotional and physical challenges.

Some authors may identify a spiritual component making the entire topic airy-fairy or supernatural. Others may cite Indigo Children's unique attributes as pathologies, and are quick to label them with an illness that is quickly followed up by a pharmaceutical prescription or therapy. Most books about Indigo Children are written by adults, not the children living it. They may ask questions of the Indigo Children and post their answers, but this is still a very limited look of living as an Indigo on a daily basis.

Our book is a firsthand rendition written by an Indigo Child and her parent, the trials, tribulations and triumphs. More importantly, this book is written from the perspective of living it and owning it, with all the power and self-esteem that Indigos should be proud to possess.

Our hope is that you will develop a greater understanding of who you really are, and why you are here at this time, and even more importantly, how to deal with the unique challenges facing us Indigos, at this time on planet Earth.

Ever since the Indigo label was applied to children, there have been mixed connotations. The original catchphrase might have been used to highlight these special youngsters, but in reality, it has just boxed them into a category of "not normal" kid.

From our personal experience, we can assure you that Indigo Children are very normal. If anything, they are super normal, in that they are us, but so much more in tune with themselves and their environment. And therein lies the challenge. Since they are so highly aware, they are also highly sensitive.

Labeling our children is noting that they are "different." Unfortunately, these labels keep them separate and isolated from each other and from us. And, the only thing that all our kids really want is to just "fit in" and "be like everyone else."

Labeling prevents them from seeing the bigger picture of who they really are, and it limits our own beliefs of who they are capable of becoming.

> *She's gifted.*
> *He's slow.*
> *She's special.*
> *He's autistic.*
> *She's so talented.*
> *He's so lazy.*
> *She's too short.*
> *He's too skinny.*

The list is endless. And if you are a parent reading this, you already know how many labels can be placed on your child.

Introduction

And if you are a child reading this, the message here is to ignore the labels placed upon you. You are already great, and you don't have to convince anyone but yourself.

When we were looking for answers to our queries about Indigo Children, we found a few books written by "experts" with little or no parenting experience, and none by an Indigo Child that hadn't been down the road of medication or institutionalization. And that is precisely the dilemma.

When one writes a book about successfully raising special children, there are two important questions that should be asked:

1. Is the author a parent raising this special child?

2. Is the author a special child who has mastered their specialness?

Luckily for us, we can answer "yes" to both questions. Of course there were many challenges along the way, but pushing through and looking for better answers than what the conventional world provided has allowed both my daughter and I not only to survive, but to thrive. And guess what? You can too.

As a parent, we need to embrace our child and find a way for her to flourish, and not just endure in this conformist world. As a parent of an Indigo, you must realize that her needs are different, not just physically, but mentally, emotionally and spiritually. The reality is that each child is remarkable in her own way, and has distinctive needs. So we need to be aware of this and listen to our own intuition. Notice the labels, but ultimately, let them go, as they will only place restrictions on your child's blossoming.

You are your child's parent. She chose you as much as you chose her. To the extent that you are here to guide and support her, she is here to enlighten you with a new paradigm of living in appreciation and gratitude; not just for the physical gifts that are yet to be rediscovered, but for the spiritual gifts that lay dormant deep within each of you; these gifts of essential consciousness and knowingness that rise up, to keep each of you moving forward, even when you may face that dark night of the soul.

This paradigm of comprehending your inner wisdom in this materialistic world can jolt your understanding and perception of reality to an unparalleled stratum that is almost impossible to envision. My Indigo Child has enlightened my life and my world in ways that I could never have imagined. She has helped me find not only my physical health but my spiritual health as well, touching my core with an intensity of perceptive knowing.

Our story could very well be your story. Although each child is unique and brings her own inherent resources, we do this as parents as well. Once tapped into, these intrinsic gifts will unfold with authenticity, and enrich not just the immediate family, but the entire community at large. We need to respect these offerings by nurturing not just our own child, but everyone's child.

Indigos bring with them such a deep sense of wisdom and intelligence. When they speak, you wonder how such young

Introduction

children can be that insightful. And when they are quiet, you wonder how they could be that deeply hurt.

When each of us incarnated, we vibrated with our own intrinsic magnificence. We were all born perfect, whole and complete. So how did we end up here? In this place of disconnect from who we really are?

This book will help remind you that the part of you which is perfect, whole and complete, is still there. It is somewhere within, hidden under the indoctrinated philosophies of your family, friends and teachers. Weighed down by the responsibilities and problems of others, and the burdens of day to day life, you may not only have lost your health, you may actually have lost you way. . . your way to think, your way to live, and your way to just be in your joy and happiness. You are perfect, whole and complete. You just got sidetracked and forgot.

We offer the discovery of realizing that you are unique with all of the associated responsibilities and possibilities. Who are you capable of becoming? And will you, can you, move forward in that direction, knowing that you are the forerunner in that arena. When you realize that you are never truly alone, when you know that the Universe is supporting you, will you get out of your comfort zone, and move forward fearlessly?

Of course your friends may think you're irrational, maybe weird or perhaps even crazy. But you must realize that their opinion is just that – their opinion, and has absolutely nothing to do with who you really are. Each of us must walk our own walk regardless of the limiting beliefs others have instilled upon us. The journey is the adventure, and the destination is just another rest station until the next destination. We need to be true to ourselves and live life in all our own glory.

We aspire to open the eyes of parents who are overwhelmed with psychological diagnostic labels and medications given to their children; and to enlighten the children that they too can finally feel comfortable in their own skin. Earth really is our home planet, and we just have to fine tune the way that we live here to really thrive. Success is within reach if we keep an open mind to possibilities outside of society's customary way of thinking.

Indigos are here to stay. They are the doctors, lawyers, and professionals of tomorrow. They will be our teachers, the parents of our grandchildren, and perhaps even our caretakers as we enter into our later years. No amount of medical diagnosing, drugs or therapy will make them disappear. This new onslaught of learning disabilities, ADD, ADHD and autism in great proportion of our children, is, we believe, a manifestation of society's inability to recognize that there is indeed, a new wave of children who require a different kind of parenting than what is conventional.

With love, proper guidance and a holistic environment, Indigos can and will flourish into the beautiful adults that they are meant to be. Our collaboration of anecdotal stories, insights and effective healing techniques will assist you in achieving this. As we heal our children, we heal ourselves.

Now is the time.

Chapter One
* * *

In the Beginning: Mom's Story

Be not afraid of greatness: some are born great, some achieve greatness, and some have greatness thrust upon them. – William Shakespeare

By most accounts, my daughter's birth was somewhat uneventful. Coming five years after her brother, I was looking forward to her arrival. Just twelve hours of labor; not too bad considering that her older sibling took twice as long.

It was a painful and tedious labor, involving delivery by low forceps and an episiotomy. She was a mere 6 lbs 3 oz, but the delivering obstetrician said that she would have been a C-section baby if she were any larger. It was as if she was resistant to arriving into the world. A portend of what was yet to come.

She was healthy, but challenged by her first breaths. The delivery staff looked worried. My husband looked ashen. A pediatrician was called for possible CPR. Apgar was 3 (10 is healthy), and she was suctioned twice. A crash cart arrived; a DeeLee catheter was inserted to clear the breathing airway.

Finally after nearly two minutes, she gasped her first breaths. She was monitored closely for twenty four hours and given Light Therapy for the jaundice that was noted. Two days later, she was vigorous enough to be discharged.

So began the life of my Indigo baby.

Her complexion was a rosy shade of pink and her eyes were the bluest blue that I had ever seen. So blue in fact, that our babysitter insisted on referring to her as "Azul Celeste" (*Heavenly Blue* in Spanish). I thought this was endearing at the time, but years later, I discovered that this name was a hint to who she really was. Her disposition was fairly tempered and toothlessly smiley. And when she lay on her tummy, her little tush was always up in the air; a sure mark of a little girl who was showing off her good points. Yes, there was no denying it. She was my baby daughter with an attitude. Although she was the exact birth weight as her brother, she was so physically different in appearance. Her older brother was born with dark brown black eyes and an olive complexion. I was so amazed and delighted to have this beautiful angelic looking baby girl.

As naturally fresh-faced as she looked, there was something definitely not right. During her first year of life, she cried continuously. I nursed at the beginning, but this did not seem to fill her. So we supplemented with formula. Still the crying continued. The pediatrician said it was intolerance to the cow milk formula so we switched to the soy variety. This also proved to be not agreeable, as she appeared to have painful gas that kept her crying even more than before. Finally, there was goat milk- the solution to the problem.

Looking back at this, many years later, the answers are clear in my head, as hind sight is always 20/20.

Of course, she couldn't tolerate cow milk. She's a sensitive child with a sensitive digestive system. Cow isn't even the

In the Beginning: Mom's Story

same species as us. You wouldn't give your baby Monkey milk, and yet that is a lot closer to our genus than Bovine (cow) is. Does my child have four stomachs like a cow does? Of course not! The human body has a great deal of innate intelligence. It knows what resonates with good health and flourishing. And being the innately wisdomy kid that she was and still is, she knew that cow milk based formula was a no-no. As for soy, well the truth of it is clear two decades later- Milk Soy Protein Intolerance (MSPI). Unfortunately, the pediatricians weren't so smart back then.

Pre-Birth

But I wish to back up a bit, as telltale signs of her uniqueness were even apparent during my pregnancy. It was somewhere about seven weeks into gestation, when I was hit with light bleeding. Having a medical background myself, I was gripped with the fear of possible miscarriage. "Okay", I told myself, "these things happen. I will just let it be and move on."

The light bleeding lasted about two days, surely not enough for a miscarriage but certainly enough to be concerned. I redid the home pregnancy test, and it was inconclusive. I reappointed with the gynecologist and it was confirmed that indeed I was still pregnant. So what the heck was the bleeding about. As the doctor said, "These things just happen."

I was plagued with nausea throughout the pregnancy. Not just the first trimester, but the second and most of the third as well. It wasn't just a little morning sickness; it was an all day and all night sickness. So much in fact, that I had lost a lot of weight, and was threatened to be hospitalized if I didn't regain it. I would sleep every night with my head propped up on three pillows, as laying flat seemed to intensify the queasiness. When the nausea finally lightened up in the last trimester, I was able to eat fully with a tremendous craving for red meat. One week before going into labor, I had a terrible cold and sore throat. I was extremely uncomfortable, but refused medication, as I was determined to have a drug free healthy baby.

As a side note, I should also mention that I never had any ultrasound pictures taken during my pregnancy. This was my choice, even though the obstetrician had made many offers with hopes to mollify me during my never ending nausea. (Perhaps it was even an additional billable procedure for insurance). No one yet knew the long term effects of ultrasound on a developing fetus, and I didn't want my kid to be a statistic 20 years later. This baby was mine whether it was a boy, girl, healthy or not.

Eventually, my resistance wore down. I finally took two aspirin for a splitting headache and low grade fever that developed along with the respiratory cold in that last week. As fate would have it, the next day, the labor started.

When we arrived at the hospital, it was quite crowded. It seemed that everyone in New York City was in labor that night and attention from the medical staff was extremely limited. After many hours of painful labor and exhaustive Hee-Hee blow breathing, I was lucky enough to finally meet with the anesthesiologist for an epidural. Too bad the anesthesia didn't last long enough for the actual delivery. The entire labor affair actually seemed surreal at the time. But that may have had something to do with the very full moon that was hovering in the sky that evening. The only thing that seemed to be missing that night was the howling of werewolves in the background, although the screaming of the excessive number (twenty eight) of women in labor was probably a close second. Either way, by 7:45AM, my bundle of joy was here. Other than her breathing challenge and a large strawberry hemangioma on her left hip, she was perfect.

Early Childhood

I should make it clear that my daughter was not always a psychically gifted child. Actually she was pretty much a regular kid, in public school, going to typical extracurricular programs in sports, music and art. She was exceptionally bright, and definitely a caring soul with a big heart. She always had something nice to say to everybody with that beautiful childhood innocence.

I remember when she was about 3 years old; she was watching me get dressed to go to work. I was somewhat frenzied as I was running late and she just blurted out, "Mommy, you look so beautiful." Her eyes were big and bright and so full of love. This simple statement hit me hard. How many three year olds do you know come out with an endearing comment like that, unprovoked? Not the three year olds that I know.

She would have the usual play dates with her friends, and nothing supernatural was ever happening. She never saw angels or dead people anywhere, and was never afraid to sleep in her own room due to any entities being there. This being said, the only unusual thing that I ever noticed about her, was her deep empathy for anyone in need, and her ability to feel "off" after being with certain people who were just not nice people. This clairsentience on her part, was not really anything unusual, as I think most of us have had similar feelings ourselves, after we've been in the presence of energy draining personalities. But this one trait was the foundation from which all of her other traits developed in her teenage years. It is from this vantage point that I would like to discuss some of the events that I believe created the shifts within her that exponentially grew into multi-dimensional psychic gifts.

At the age of one, my daughter had the first of several febrile seizures. Another one at the age of two and a half, five and then at the age of eleven!!! I emphasize the age eleven because it is unusual for any child to have a febrile seizure past the age of five. Surely something else must have been going on in her nervous system that no doctor had yet put a diagnosis on.

The episodes all started out the same; she always seemed perfectly normal, and then within a short period of time, typically in less than one hour, her temperature would elevate to 103 degrees or more. There was usually no warning about this. She would suddenly just start to feel sick and then she would lose consciousness and have a convulsion, along with the high fever.

Just to clarify to those who may be reading this, febrile seizures are an extremely dangerous and scary event that can be deadly if the fever is not controlled quickly. A visit to the emergency room afterwards always validated some plausible bacterial infection that would be treated with an antibiotic.

In the Beginning: Mom's Story

And of course there would be several days of Advil and Tylenol in three hour alternating sequences to make sure that the fever would not again spike up suddenly. Most kids outgrow febrile seizures by the age of five. Why then did my child have one at the ripe old age of eleven?

There was one other event that I believe had a significant impact on my daughter's life, and her developing her sixth sense abilities.

When my daughter was about 3 years old, I contracted Lyme disease. This is a very insidious infection, that can be difficult to diagnose, and if left untreated, can be progressively debilitating and ultimately fatal. There wouldn't be much of a story to tell except that I was one of the unlucky ones who did not get accurately diagnosed at the onset. However, when I was properly diagnosed two years after contracting this illness, much damage was already done to my physical and mental health, and I was not a well person. My symptoms were similar to late stages of Multiple Sclerosis, in that I had major neurological, muscular, brain and cardiac dysfunction. I could barely stand, as my muscles seemed to not function at all, no matter how much I wanted them too. The road to recovery was slow and disappointing, and at times, hopeless. Seven years into this unrelenting illness, my physician said that I should seriously consider selling my practice and go on permanent disability, as there truly seemed to be no end in sight.

So, when my daughter was five years old and in kindergarten, we had a problem. While I was fully disabled due to the Lyme disease and pretty much bedbound with an

IV line hanging out of my arm, my daughter was having her own challenges at school.

Diandra had a young, fresh, highly erudite teacher with very little actual classroom experience. This teacher loved to exert her authority by reprimanding the little children who misbehaved. Actually, my daughter was never meant to be the direct recipient of the teacher's yelling. However, Diandra would emotionally cower inside when the teacher would have her screaming fest at some other classmate. Ultimately, this created a great deal of anxiety in my child that would usually manifest in her emotionally recoiling and then wetting herself. Up till this point, my child was fully potty trained since the age of two.

And to add insult to injury, this self-grandeurized teacher suggested that my daughter should be moved into a slower class for the next year as she obviously was not "gifted" enough to be in this enriched(???) program. Prior to enrolling in this class, Diandra was always a star pupil in nursery and preschool, with an inquisitive congenial personality. She was given a standard IQ test before kindergarten started, by an examiner with over thirty years experience testing children, and the results were that "Diandra possesses superior intellectual capacity" with a rating at "98th percentile as compared with other children of her age." She "always reacted well to praise and encouragement." She "expressed her ideas clearly and in good detail, maintained interest and was always responsive and cooperative" and "would profit from placement in a class with an enriched curriculum."

So how did we end up like this? In an "enriched program" that was more keen on intimidating the children into intellectual submission rather than praising them into their own greatness. Obviously there was really nothing "enriching" about this program at all.

The option of moving Diandra to another class with a more nurturing teacher was presented mid school year and followed through. The wetting stopped but the emotional scarring was already in place. She had become more shy and reclusive, leading to her being ignored by teachers who had their hands full with the more boisterous kids. My beautiful gifted angelic child was then put on the regular school track with kids who were behavior problems, had learning disabilities or struggled with English as a Second Language (ESL). She was somewhat happier in this new school setup, but was treated like an outsider by the friends that she had left behind in the "gifted" program. Yet she was also an outsider to her new classmates who had very different dispositions than she had. Actually, her best friends in elementary school turned out to be the ESL children who tended to show more respect for education than any of the others.

These early years were very difficult for Diandra, as she continued to have challenges with school, and continued to worry that Mom was going to die from this horrible Lyme disease that no one could cure. At one point, at the age of five, she totally refused to go to school at all. She said that she wanted to be home in case I needed help, and if she did go to school, it would be her fault if I died since she wasn't there to help me. It was heart wrenching for me to see her feel this way. Eventually, after a year of family therapy, her belief system shifted and we no longer had this emotional issue to deal with.

When Diandra was in fifth grade, I finally managed to rid myself of Lyme disease, but I still was not well. This was due to damage from the Lyme disease itself and additionally due to the side effects of massive amounts of experimental medications that I had taken for those seven years. Doctors had no cure for my lingering symptoms of fatigue, brain fog, tremors and neuropathy. More medication was the only option offered, but I wasn't going down that path again.

It wasn't until five years later that I finally came upon the solutions to my lingering symptoms as well as the understanding of Diandra's path.

Insights

It was at Diandra's age of fifteen, that the blinds were finally opened and the light was beginning to come in with some answers to my daughter's life journey as well as the answer to my own life journey. At that time, I was new to the world of Energy Medicine, and an associate of mine enthusiastically recommended that I take a metaphysical healing course in Denver, Colorado. The idea of going there alone was not very appealing. Firstly, since I had many lingering health challenges from chronic Lyme disease, and was somewhat afraid to travel alone and be on my own.

Secondly, I didn't want to be with a bunch of "crazies," two thousand miles away from home. My colleague convinced me that taking my daughter might be comforting, and that my husband and son could join us later in the week for a family vacation. Well, when you presented it that way, it didn't seem so bad. Besides, I had never been to Denver and a vacation was definitely in order.

In the Beginning: Mom's Story

The course turned out to be a real eye opener. Not just for the greater understanding of Energy Medicine in general, but also for the revelations about my daughter's life path. Until this point, everyone knew her to be a normal loving sensitive child who was conventionally grounded in the here and now. So what I am about to tell you about what happened next, was unsettling to me at that time, but perfectly positioned in retrospect.

The four day meeting consisted mostly of lay people trying to heal their own illnesses, but there were also some medical people in the group of about sixty. My daughter was the only child present. The instructor of the seminar asked her and the only pediatrician in the group to come up front for an experiential demonstration.

Diandra sat in a chair, and the pediatrician put one hand on her forehead and the other hand on the back of her head. It didn't look like much, and was actually pretty boring from the audience perspective. My daughter was nervous but smiling as she just sat there with her eyes closed. But after about five to six minutes, something shifted. Suddenly she just burst out hysterically crying and then the demonstration was over.

She said that she wasn't really sure what it was she was crying about but there was something about "darkness and being left behind." The pediatrician was obviously an intuitive and he said that he saw that she was a twin in utero and that her twin abruptly left her there - in utero.

Now there was an interesting concept, I had been pregnant with twins and didn't even know it! Floodgates opened up in my mind and I knew instinctively that the bleeding that I had at the beginning of the pregnancy was indeed a miscarriage, a miscarriage of my daughter's twin.

My daughter was a bit unsettled after this meeting, but soon she regained her composure. However, the repercussions of her being a twin have played out over and over throughout the following years. As we traveled into other metaphysical circles, intuitives and psychics have continued to point out that she was indeed, a twin.

Now this would be the end of the twin narrative, but the chronicles of her long lost twin continued to develop and get more interesting as time went on. It was during my daughter's freshman year in college that I ended up meeting her twin in a very life changing dream. It was January of her freshman year. I went to sleep as usual and dreamt myself into the middle of a great expansiveness of stars. There was a road of light rays that lay arched out in front of me. On my left, was a beautiful young dark haired woman who almost seemed like a powerful goddess. On my right was a young man with thick wavy blond hair. Next to him was my daughter. Both were of the same age and the two almost looked like each other in their coloring and facial structure. Further down on the right, was my son with his recognizable dark features.

My eyes seemed to see everyone and everything in that dream world with pure crystal clarity. The woman on my left asked me "Do you have fear?" and my answer was "Yes, but not really." She kept repeating that I should "Go past the fear." again and again. The three young people on my right just watched quietly, and supportively looked on at me with deep tender loving affection. There was a tremendous feeling of unrestrained freedom in the dream, and I seemed to radiate just pure love, health, and healing light from my chest. I remember waking up crying and trying to regain my composure, still feeling this expansive feeling in my chest. I quickly wrote the dream down, since I had a feeling that this was a very meaningful vision, and I didn't want to forget any of it.

The next day I called my daughter who was away at college, and I told her that I thought that the young man in my dream was the man she would probably marry one day, and that I would recognize him in a heartbeat if I ever met him. We gossiped on like two girlfriends to see if she knew anyone who might vaguely resemble him, as we certainly didn't want Mr. Right to be missed. There were some possibilities, but nothing seemed to fit the bill.

It was in May that the truth of the matter finally presented itself. Diandra had just finished her freshman year, and was finally home to enjoy her summer. We started out talking about the many challenges of living in the dorm with hundreds of hormonally imbalanced PMS young women, and having to subsist on poor quality cafeteria food. Being energetically sensitive, she had to clear herself constantly from EVERYTHING all the time, and it really took its toll on her health as well as her studies. After deep consideration, she decided not to continue with this college, but to move back home and commute to a local university.

After this monumental decision was reached, we broached the subject of friends and when or if her true soulmate was really ever going to show up. From here we opened up the topic of that dream that I had in January. Diandra went into her Universal Communicator position and directly asked the Higher Consciousness of the guy in the dream "Who are you?" We were both surprised to find out that he was not her Mr. Right at all, but was in fact her twin that everyone had been speaking about for the last three years!

From there she went on to ask him other questions; what was his name, why he left her and where he was now. I will keep the answers short as Diandra will discuss this in a later chapter. Basically, his name is Azul (*Blue* in Spanish), he escorted her into this realm because she didn't come willingly due to fear of previous life persecution, he left her in utero once she was in place, and right now he is acting as her guide until he reincarnates, probably as one of my grandchildren.

The Sixth Sense Developed

That trip to Colorado was the turning point of her awakening. At first, I didn't take Diandra to many metaphysical classes since the bulk of them were in our area, and I could easily travel there by myself. Besides, she had school which took priority; and personally, that whole twin thing that happened at the front of the class in Colorado sort of left her a little uncomfortable with the entire idea of metaphysical healing.

However, I continued to go to a diverse array of energy healing classes regularly. Within a year, I had cured myself of fibromyalgia as well as a lot of other chronic "incurable" little symptoms. My daughter was amazed. I was literally a new woman. I was Mom with energy and vitality, and since she actually had no memory of me ever being that, this was a miracle! She wanted to learn what I had learned and I was more than happy to have my beautiful angelic child be by my side learning with me.

When I think back on that first course we took together in Colorado, the year before, I recall one of the assistants in the group had told us something very profound that still resonates with me today. He said "Of all the possible pairings in the energy field, the pairing of mother and daughter is the most powerful." He said it beat husband-wife, brother-sister and any other combination that you could think of. At the time, I didn't make much of it, but here we are years later, and we do make an amazing team in our energy healing together.

As a team, Diandra and I registered for a reflexology class together, and then she independently moved on to a sound therapy class. From there, it was Reiki and then The Reconnection. It was here when things started to evolve. Somewhere after The Reconnection, at the age of sixteen, she was able to start seeing guides. And the rest, they say, is history.

In Retrospect

I remember back to when I was growing up. I was the youngest of five children, and the only girl. I was raised to believe that girls were inferior; they grow up, and if they are lucky, find a husband and have children. It was the 60s and I was taught to see the world from a very different vantage point.

Something inside me knew that this was wrong. Perhaps it was because I was the youngest, and I saw everyone before me mess up their lives, or perhaps it was because I was the only girl in a family of boys and saw how my own mother was mistreated, or perhaps it was because I was born with an innate wisdom that stuck, no matter what anyone said. Or maybe it was because I was an airy Libra with a stubborn Taurus rising. Although I was raised to be a nobody, I kept my own vision. I did well in school, attained accolades, and paved my own way through college and dental school.

I can still recall so many people telling me I couldn't go to college, shouldn't go to dental school. "Girls don't do that. Girls get married and have children. And maybe, just maybe if they are lucky, they might marry a doctor. But definitely, they don't become one. Oh, and of course, it's such a dirty job to be in people's mouth. You should be a nurse instead." Oh sure, cleaning bedpans is so much more sanitary.

I tell you this story not to gloat, but to instill in you that everyone has a dream, a vision of whom they can be, and it is up to you and me and each of us to assist our children to be on their own distinctive path to joy, happiness and integrity. And if we can do this with genuine love and admiration, ascension on all levels, and for each of us, is assured.

Chapter Two
* * *
In the Beginning: Diandra's Story

Those who seek to find their inner passion will always succeed. Find your true gifts within and the Light will guide you. – Azul, Diandra's Twin of the Light

I remember a white yellow light glaring over my body. The room's temperature was warm. A goopy slime covered my mouth, and nose. The doctors suctioned my nose and mouth. I wanted to scream out, but the glop was in my lungs.

There was an angel draped in white light in the room positioned by the entryway. She was a tall woman that seemed to stand over everyone. She had blue heavenly eyes that when I looked at them, I could feel a rush of peace encompass my whole being.

I was still not able to take the first breath of life. I could feel my body going cold and numb. I was going home.

After a little longer than nine months, trapped in my body shell, I was going to able to go back to the light. I could hear the faint sound of beeping, steadily trying to take account of my baby body.

Something suctioned my nose and mouth again. But this time it was a deeper suction that went all the way down to my lungs.

I was back. My loss of consciousness was no more.

I took a deep breath and wailed out loud. I heard small cheers from the people that were holding me. The energy had shifted in the room; it was calmer. The angel waved her hand goodbye and evaporated in white golden light.

My umbilicus was cut; I started to cry again. I was put in a warm blanket and then handed over to my mom. She was tired. I could tell since the energy had dropped from her face. My maternal grandfather was watching us. He had passed away several years before. My maternal grandmother beckoned my grandfather to the light. He too left in white golden light and vanished from the room.

My mom handed me over to my dad, who was sitting. My paternal grandfather, the one I am named after, was standing over my dad. My grandfather waved and then smiled at me. He too left in white golden light and vanished from the room.

This above recollection is from the first moments after my birth. I channeled it in from my Newborn Higher Self for greater accuracy. Personally and presently, I really don't remember any of it. Yet I could clairvoyantly see it all, as if it were happening now.

Pre- Birth

But these thoughts bring me back a few years, before I was even a glint in my parent's eyes. Prior to incarnating into this lifetime, I was a non-physical being. Think hologram. I remembered all my past lives, people I had met, places I had lived, life lessons I needed to pursue, karmic lessons to learn. Everything.

Then, when I was born on this earthly plane, I sort of forgot all that stuff. I say "sort of forgot," since I actually can remember everything, but only if I channel it from the consciousness of my own memory.

For me, I liked "life" before I incarnated. I obviously did not want to be born, which is a major reason why being born was such a complex effort. Before incarnation, I was a free spirit. My existence was good. There was no language barrier. Honesty was customary, as lying was an implausible possibility. I know that this Universal Language will eventually exist on earth, as some of us Indigos are already using it to communicate with each other. It is an evolutionary process that will play itself out for those who are ready to accept it.

Energetically, I understood myself better then, since I remembered all my lives and lessons. As my spiritual self, I was able to choose when and where I would incarnate, which country I would live in, if I would be male or female, my parents and all the experiences that I would undertake.

I chose my parents as a result of the lessons that I needed to learn and to grow as a soul. It might sound foolish to purposely choose people that I may not get along with, or face stressful events that are painful, but these lessons are needed for spiritual growth and for moving forward towards enlightenment.

Although it may be hard to believe, a child gets to decide who their parents are before they are born into a family. So if you find that you don't see eye to eye with your mom or dad, just remember that you chose them.

Sometimes the child can also pick their siblings. This is not a lottery, or who has the best stuff. These family members are based on karmic contracts -basically who you know in a previous life and what lessons need to be learned on either party's end. If the karmic contract or the lesson to be learned was not mastered in that life with a certain person, place or thing, then you have to meet that person or have certain obstacles again and again until they complete the course.

Before my mom came down in human form, she and I made an agreement that she would create the path and I would come later as her backup person; almost like we had a mission together for mutual support. I know that she has paved the way for me, putting the footprints in the sand, and for this I am eternally grateful. She has laid the foundation so that I can thrive with all my sensitivities and abilities that conventional society labels as a disability or illness. If I had a different mother, my life may have taken an entirely different spin.

When the time was getting closer to take a human form on the earthly plane, I did not want to go. I was told by the angels that I would be fine, and that my parents would be nice. Unfortunately, the angels' words of encouragement were not enough to prompt me to go. I know that in many previous lifetimes, I was persecuted for my intuitive gifts and the fear of going through that again was palpable.

Due to my unwillingness to leave the etheric spiritual world, a soul stepped forward and volunteered to come with me. Now that didn't seem so bad. At least I was going to have an ally who would be there to keep me company and support me. He introduced himself as "Azul." He said he would come down with me and be my twin.

Even with the many known perks of incarnating (appealing to the 5 senses of taste, touch, auditory, olfactory, sight), I was still resistant to being born. A deal was made. Azul had agreed to be my twin. I had no idea that the bigger plan was for Azul to escort me in utero and then leave before I was born.

Remember I said that when we incarnate, we forget our past lives, our purpose and any secrets to life. So when we made this deal, I was not thinking like an experienced soul that had incarnated before; instead I was thinking like a scared new soul with trepidations of incarnating. Luckily, Azul took on the job with ease and reassurance, like an old pro. I learned later that I had helped him incarnate too, in the very same way in many other previous lives. Apparently we had "twinned" each other in many lifetimes before, providing mutual support.

In retrospect, when I found out about Azul, and that I was conceived as a twin, many aspects of my growing up years seemed to make sense; like how easily I seem to attract twins into my life, why my babysitter called me Azul Celeste (Heavenly Blue), that my rising sign is in Gemini (The Twins), why I always felt like there was a part of me that was missing.

And now that I am able to talk to Azul, I routinely ask him questions. These were my basics:

If you were able to leave, why was I not able to?
You did not know how.

What is our relationship now; you are obviously not my twin?
I can be referred to as Azul, the Twin of the Light.

What is your purpose?
My (Azul's) purpose is to guide you and your family and to help with communication between your realm and the angels, ascended masters etc.

What is my purpose?
It is defined by many aspects. First there are your life lessons you need to overcome. Then there is the change and support you need to provide for your family and the world.

It has taken some deep soul searching and some energetic clearing, but I have finally gotten over the sorrow and grief of being left behind by Azul to fend for myself in a callous unyielding society. But presently, Azul serves a guide for me, giving me insights to managing my life here. I may have lost what might have been my closest friend and sibling, but have gained so much more on an entirely different level. For this I am grateful.

Early Childhood

For most Indigos, the intuitive component is spotted at an early age. This can manifest as having imaginary friends, or seeing passed-away family members or communicating with pets. Most people think that all Indigos can see people's aura or past-lives by age five. I couldn't do any of this. What most people do not realize is that there are other traits that signify an Indigo. (See Chapter 3 for Indigo Attributes). It is also important to realize that intuitive abilities may not manifest when the person is a small child.

My mom often says that when I was little, she felt like she was talking to someone older, even though I was only a little kid at the time. When I think back to those moments and of what I said and why I said it, it felt like all I was doing was speaking the truth. My words only sounded wise because they were honest words. Most people do not speak the truth. They usually place their own spin on the words they speak so as to further their own agenda. It is all about what they can gain, who they can manipulate, not about helping others. So for me, my key Indigo manifestations were emotional/physical sensitivity and innate wisdom.

Sensitivity and wisdom in a young child is <u>not</u> something that society values or respects. My parents knew that I was exceptional and they have always valued my intelligence and fundamental nature. And for this, I am deeply thankful. I know that almost all parents think their kid is special, but my parents always treated me so.

Sensitive kids (grownups too) are usually aware of how others are feeling emotionally and tune into them. In my case, in kindergarten, whenever the teacher would yell at other students I would cry. I was feeling the bullied kid's emotion. To go further into the memory of my kindergarten days, the teacher would get so intense that I would actually wet my clothes. Even now while I am writing this I feel the embarrassment rising in me. But then I remember I was only five years old. Young children need to be in a nurturing environment. Unfortunately the schools are not perfect and there are no hidden cameras watching the classroom. My teacher was a young and unhappy soul, so this is how she let it vent.

I want to say that although I was trying to remember how my teacher got intense I could not recall at all what she said. All I could remember was that she would start to yell at a classmate, I would cringe and shake all over, and then I would wet myself. I guess I blocked out the middle part of the story.

To remember what the teacher did to my fellow student I etherically read my Regular Self when I was five to get the answer:

Her face turned red; she was in Jake's face. She was two inches away. Her aura was a fiery red with snakes swirling around; she looked like the evil Medusa. Jake's aura all around him was different hues of brown.

It is interesting to hear my five-year-old voice describe the event since I was not an intuitive then. But I could definitely "feel" something going on.

To this day, I still am emotionally and physically sensitive, especially with school matters. If a teacher speaks harshly to me, I can feel the tears well up in my eyes. My mom always said, "Just because they are teachers, it doesn't mean that they're nice people or highly intelligent." And she is so right.

They are just like you or me and they may just be having a bad day or maybe they are emotionally unstable or inherently ignorant. That being said, I want to mention that I have also had some amazingly loving wonderful teachers as well. It's just that the mean ones really stick out in my memory and can affect us sensitive Indigos on a very deep level.

Another scenario of sensitivity that I remember is when I simply would go and sit with those who were upset. This is not really a good thing as us Indigos will tend to pick up the emotions of the other person. This could be quite ungrounding and leave us in a bad place after the encounter. I know even now that if a family member is angry, I will avoid them so that I won't feel horrible afterward. I know that my sheer presence will make them feel better but I need to protect myself. (See Chapter 7 for protection tools). Too bad I didn't know this when I was younger.

A big part of my childhood memories focus on when my mom was stricken with Lyme disease. This was a tough time, not just for me, but for my entire family. My mom has always been the center of our family, so when she wasn't right, I wasn't right. When someone you love is physically, emotionally or spiritually sick, it can be hard for anyone to cope, but even more so for an Indigo. For me, this happened when I was three years old.

I know that most conventional people say that children do not have memories from age three. Well, they are wrong. I remember my mom laying in her bed with a long needle and tubes sticking out of her arm; when my mom would get a new experimental medicine to try and she would experience the mood changes and horrible side effects; I remember the long drives the family would take to a special doctors for her treatment; and I especially remember the quiet talks that both my mom and dad would have about the possibility of my mom dying. Her disease lasted many years of my early life, and I can feel all the anxiety, fear and overwhelming sadness flooding through me. I also remember refusing to go to school for the fear that my mom would die without me.

It was a hard time, and I think that having gone through this has made me a better person. My mom has often said that I helped her tremendously during those years, as I gave her a reason to push through and carry on and continue to want to get well. At an older age, she has even credited me with helping her to get her on the right path to refinding her health just by my saying the right things at the right time. I am thankful to have been there for her, and I am indebted that this has brought me to my life's path of going into the healing arts.

Looking back at my childhood years, I see that there was a reason for everything that happened. Sure, I may not have liked it at the time, but there were lessons that needed to be learned and sometimes these lessons don't come easily.

And this brings me to my history with my many febrile seizures. No one in my family has a history of this, so I know that I was not genetically predisposed to getting them. So what was the point? The only febrile seizure that I blatantly remember was at age 11.

I remember that I wasn't even sick. Then I had a low grade fever. The fever would seem relatively stable and then it would suddenly spike high to over 102 degrees F. It was not the high fever that seemed to cause the seizure but the speed of the spike itself. From the spike, my eyes would roll back into my head and I would pass out.

Later in life, I asked many etheric sources why it was it that I had these seizures. The universal response was that a type of rewiring of my brain was necessary so that I would be able to handle higher intuitive capabilities. There are other ways for this to occur but apparently, this was my path for evolving.

Being an intuitive with the type of ability or strength that you have, takes a certain intensity and re-awakening of the brain to apply the intuitive gift. Neurons have to vibrate on a distinct wavelength,– channeled through Universal Consciousness of the Light.

In my experience, I have noticed that there are a rising number of young children who are having febrile seizures. Surely the new children being born are much more sensitive to EVERYTHING and this evolutionary shift is affecting them deeply.

Insights

When my clients ask about Indigos, they would somehow come to the assumption, that I had this perfect childhood. They assume that I had lots of friends and did well in school, that the teachers loved me, and I never had to deal with bullies. Actually by most accounts, I should get 100% on all my exams since all I have to do is channel in the correct information from the right resources and it's a no brainer. Now THAT is funny!

The key to remember is that Indigos are still human, just with an extra innate sixth (perhaps even seventh, eighth and more) sense. We have lessons to learn, have karma to deal with and obstacles to overcome.

The perceived difference between us and everyone else is an illusion. There is no difference. And when the masses realize this, there will be no labels put upon us. Let us just celebrate that we each have our own talents to share with each other. You may be a natural with the violin; well I think that's a great gift. Well, I am a natural with Universal Communication. Be as happy for me as I am for you.

Just like you, I need a nurturing loving holistic environment to thrive. I cannot eat junk food and expect to be healthy; and neither should you. The only difference is that my body and mind are a lot more sensitive to the environment, and I will be more messed up (out of balance) than non-Indigos. Hence, the diagnoses of learning disabled, ADD, ADHD, autism, etc. are being used to label us out of balance Indigos.

In Retrospect

When I was younger, I kept having racial and cultural challenges with classmates. Having grown up in NYC, the melting pot of the world, one would think that this would be a non sequitur. But alas, people anywhere can be very narrow minded and judgmental. I was outcast and labeled because of my skin tone (too white), my religion (not Christian), and my being female (especially in Karate class).

And then I went to a small town college, thinking that perhaps people would be a little more mellow, welcoming and inviting. But once again, I found that peers would ostracize me since I was not a cigarette smoking, alcohol drinking co-ed. I didn't go to Christian Bible study (not my religion) like the quiet kids, and I didn't fit in with the high maintenance bleached blonde, heavy makeup, boy chasing girls. I did find some friends but their constant questions of my religion and healthy food habits always had me on guard.

So with much channeling, soul searching and talking to my mom long distance (the phone bill was tremendous), I discovered that my lesson was to show compassion and love for those who were dishing out all this hate. I would send them love and imagine white light around these people, put them in bubbles of goodness and watch them float away. Or I would find three nice things about the person; their hair, shirts, shoes, handwriting, dancing skills, or whatever. I did these exercises every day. It worked pretty well and kept things at bay, but ultimately it got too annoying to constantly keep up barriers for protection.

Surely there must be a better way than this. School is for an education, but these were not academic lessons. When I expressed my concerns about my college life to my family and friends they would justify why I should stay at that school. They put forward comments about how I should have that "away from home" college experience; that I already got a scholarship and I would be wasting it; that I would be missing out on the social scene; or some nonsense about not being academically successful like my brother who went away for college. Since these comments did not seem just or reasonable enough to stay at a college where I had to defend the true essence of me, I took the subtle hint and moved on to a different school path that was not such a social confrontation.

The point is that sometimes we have to make decisions that do not always mesh with others' plans for you; that it is alright to take another course. As my mom's favorite poet would say:

Two roads diverged in a wood, and I--
I took the one less traveled by,
And that has made all the difference.
    -Robert Frost, The Road Not Taken (1915)

So even though almost everyone thought I was crazy to give up the conventional college path, I find that my spirit is now better than ever.

What I have learned with all this is that we are never alone. There are many unseen energies and forces around us that are here to support each of us, but only if we utilize them. If I continue to believe in myself no matter what anyone says to me or about me, I will be fine. And so will you. Just believe.

You are a miracle. Know it.

Chapter Three
* * *

Am I an Indigo?

It is never too late to be who you might have been.
– George Eliot

"Indigo" refers to a new paradigm of human being. It implies a consciousness awakening and a revolutionizing of our awareness. This expression "Indigo Child," was first brought about by Nancy Tappe in the late 1960s.

Nancy Tappe is an internationally known psychic who possesses an unusual sensory condition called synesthesia. It allows her to *see* colors and *taste* shapes. Synesthesia denotes a person having a sense which can perceive additional characters, supposedly to be perceived only by other senses.

An example of this would be when a man sees blue; he also feels sweetness in his mouth. Or instead of hearing a sound like you or I might, he might see it as a color or shape in addition to, or instead of, hearing it. And every letter and number may possibly have a color or a gender.

I know this sounds weird but it is no stranger than having a sixth sense. Conventional societal norms consider synesthesia a disease. Others might consider it an enriched sensory perception (ESP in a higher vibration).

Through her condition, Nancy Tappe was able to see a consistent color around certain people, mostly children. This started in the late 1960s and early 1970s. She referred to this as their life color, created by their personal electromagnetic energy field. This perceived color was a combination between blue and violet, and eventually was referred to as Indigo. She then noticed that people with this Indigo color had certain characteristics and traits.

She went on to say that the Indigo represents the entire range of humanity. There is no "one size fits all" mentality for the Indigo personality, just as there is no "one size fits all" description for all people. Consequently, there is no one single best type of education, type of lifestyle, type of approach, etc. with these individuals. After all, within the next hundred years, practically everyone will be Indigo. And while humanity will be very different from who has existed in the past, there is just not one single approach to the Indigo mindset or personality.[1]

Indigo Attributes

When I first heard the term Indigo, I had no clue it was me. My mom came across some material saying that for Indigos, the "symptoms" (like in a syndrome or illness) that I was having were quite common. I, on the other hand dismissed what she was saying. This was due to the implication that although Indigos could be quite fantastic, they were also "double edged swords"(implying that Indigos hurt ourselves as well as those around us), and could be quite difficult to raise and almost impossible to "handle".

The amount of putting down and belittling that the term Indigo implied was nothing you would want to touch with a ten foot pole. And I certainly didn't want to be labeled as a problem child. I did not want to be associated with a term that implied that I had a learning disability or that I was a new "breed" of human.   -Diandra

We personally find that the vast majority of literature about these highly gifted children seems to lean towards the problems with Indigos. It's almost as if there is a twisted thinking that Indigos need to be "managed", like animals or novelties, not cherished as a loving child. Since the information on who qualifies as an Indigo was pretty much determined by non-Indigo people, we decided to go directly to the source.

The Universal Consciousness of Light and Love for Indigos is a collective of ascended masters, humans, angels, archangels, and guides who are here to give guidance and assurance to Indigos. They are here to help us, and especially if we call on them.

So that is exactly what we did. We asked them directly: *How does one know if one is an Indigo?*

Indigos feel everything deeply in their soul; when the emotion of one feels like the emotion of thousands. There is an instant knowing, intuitively. We are all one. Indigos know this.   - The Universal Consciousness of Light and Love for Indigos

Below is a list of Indigo attributes channeled in from *The Universal Consciousness of Light and Love for Indigos:*

1. Heart centered when young
2. Care about others more than they care about themselves
3. Wise beyond their years
4. Do not want to be here on Earth
5. Have insights about things they shouldn't have a clue about; such as deceased people, future events, past lives, etc.
6. Have an inner knowing that may be seen as arrogance by the general population of non-Indigos
7. Have imaginary friends, see angels, deceased people
8. Talk to their pets like they would talk to humans
9. Tend to hang out with nature and pets more than people
10. Crave nature. They will drag you to the park, beach, etc.
11. Have night terrors; even before they can talk
12. Have food allergies, especially to dairy, sugar and processed foods
13. Can sense evil or bad people
14. Pick up other people's emotions
15. Can get offended easily
16. Can get seizures easily
17. Can get high fevers easily
18. Use the phrase "I know." a lot
19. They are more creative and right brain dominant than most people; into artsy things- music, painting, beading, cooking, photography, etc.
20. Can be distracted easily
21. Badger parents to change for the better, in terms of giving up bad habits; smoking, alcohol, poor foods, etc.

22. Can get sick easily, only because their systems are more sensitive
23. Can have extremes in weight: very thin or very heavy
24. Stubborn
25. Prone to insomnia
26. Prone to anxiety or unfounded fears
27. Very friendly but don't have many close friends due to feelings of being different/weird
28. Find solace in being alone

Chances are that if you have the majority of these characteristics, you are probably an Indigo. Your age is not a factor, as Indigos have been here for thousands of years. Except now, there has been a tremendous Indigo population increase within the last thirty years. Not only are their numbers increasing, but so too are their abilities and sensitivities.

Truths and Myths

There seems to be a tremendous amount of conflicting information about Indigos, so we thought we would discuss some of the most prevalent statements said about Indigos.

1. *Indigos are psychic.*
   Anyone can be psychic. Actually all newborns are very intuitive but through time and discipline, this ability gets turned off.
2. *Indigos have an Indigo aura.*
   For those of us who can see auras, this is definitely not true. Catch an Indigo when she's happy or sad. Their color will change, just like anybody else. Aura

is a totally different thing than the life color that Nancy Tappe spoke about.

3. *Indigos have emotional or mental disorders: depression, ADD, ADHD, Autism, social ineptness.*
   This can really make us feel like we're defective. These disorders are just society's way to label us so that we can be "managed" with therapy or medications. This may be a way for the pharmaceutical companies to make us feel dependent on them.

4. *Indigos are children and usually under the age of 30.*
   We know many adults who are Indigos. They can be any age; not just children. Indigo souls have been born on Earth for a long time. The older Indigos are the forerunners. Their primary goal is, and was, to make sure it would be safe when more Indigos started coming.

5. *Indigos are not able to handle school or go to college.*
   Obviously not true. Look at us. Determination and goal setting are crucial. Create a Vision Board (see Chapter 8) and a goal plan. Watch your life shift into manifestation mode.

6. *Indigos have learning disabilities.*
   We all learn differently. Find your inherent strengths and weaknesses. The three most common learning styles are visual, auditory, and kinesthetic. To learn, we depend on our senses to process the information around us. Most people tend to use one of their senses more than the others. It is important to have yourself evaluated to find which style is best for you and master it in order to succeed in school as well as life. (See Chapter 8.)

7. *If a child has ADD, ADHD, Aspergers or learning disabilities then they must be an Indigo.*
   These kinds of issues are usually due to toxin and stimuli overload- from vaccines, processed foods, heavy metals, media, etc. (See Chapter 6.)
8. *Indigos are healers (Lightworkers) or work with people.*
   A definite maybe since most Indigos are caring and loving individuals. However, many Indigos are intolerant to people and would rather be left alone to grow into their own creative endeavors. Actually we find little tolerance for people who are stuck in an old paradigm of thinking.
9. *Indigos are loving, forgiving and gentle souls.*
   This can be true, but due to all the emotional traumas inflicted on such sensitive souls, many Indigos end up with deep seated anger and grief issues.
10. *Indigos need medication to function.*
    We need to stay away from this kind of thinking. Re-find the balance in your life. Release the emotional, mental and physical traumas, and you will heal. (See Chapters 6, 7 & 8.)
11. *Destructive children are Indigos.*
    Acting out is to be expected from anyone who has sensory overload.
12. *Autistic children are Indigos.*
    Turning inward and tuning out is to be expected from anyone who has sensory overload.
13. *Indigos have mystical magical powers.*
    Too funny. Actually my brother just walked in while I was writing and asked me to use my mystical magical powers to cure his itchy hands. Jokingly he said this, so I thought I would add it to the list. (Thanks Mike.)

14. Indigos are food sensitive thus causing behavioral and mind altering anomalies.
Sensitivities can vary especially with foods that are allergenic. Some examples are dairy, corn, soy, and wheat products. Any refined carbohydrates, processed sugars, GMOs, MSG or chemical preservatives will make us really reactive. (See Chapter 6.)

15. Indigos usually come in clusters.
An Indigo Child usually has an Indigo parent/guardian or siblings that are also Indigos. We need support in our inner circle. Since we are so sensitive, it is important that we have someone to talk to that is non-judgmental and encouraging.

16. Indigos are wise at an early age.
My mom often says that when I was little, she felt like she was talking to an adult even though I was a young child. Wisdom is not an age related phenomenon.

17. Indigos are highly sensitive to others' emotions.
So true. We need to learn protection. (See Chapter 8.)

18. Indigos tend to hang out with people who are sad or upset.
We want to save the world and help everyone who needs help, but try not to get caught up with others' downbeat emotions. It can consume us and we won't even realize it until it's out of control. I know even now that if a family member or friend is angry I will naturally just gravitate towards them, even if I am in another room. My sheer presence seems to make them feel better, but I am usually a mess afterward; my dog Celeste will do the same thing. She just seems to know when someone is upset and naturally

scouts them out, like it calls to her. I have asked her why she does this and she replied that they need her.
19. *Indigos are emotionally sensitive.*
This means that if a word of disapproval is spoken to us, we will act like the most horrific statement was said. We take EVERYTHING personally. My mom always jokes that because I have a black belt in Tae Kwon Do, that if someone touches me, they are dead, but if someone says "boo" to me, I will fall apart. We Indigos are just that sensitive- deal with it!

There is no cookie cutter template of how all Indigos are or will become. We are people first, albeit extremely sensitive ones, and require just what every other child needs – love and nurturance.

Rainbow, Crystal and Star Children

You are here to enable the divine purpose of the universe to unfold. That's how important you are. -Eckhart Tolle

We are very aware of this recent trend for categorizing Indigo Children. Personally, we have found this to be disparaging, as it seems that a hierarchy is being created. Truly, this is not the purpose of why these special children are here. Spending all this time figuring out which group you belong to and who has better abilities, is counterproductive. Our purpose is not to discern our differences but to focus on bringing in love and light.

Bad enough that conventional society has already labeled our precious children as being different, and here we go in the metaphysical circles, doing it to each other. My Indigo is no better or worse than your Rainbow, Crystal or Star Child. Get over it!

We are all one. We are all of the human race. Treasure our diversities and remove the labels. These tags only divide us and make us feel isolated. Honor that we are all here at this time to support each other and assist in raising our vibration into the new era of enlightenment.

[1]Tappe, Nancy. "Indigo Classification." *All About Indigos*. 2010. Web. <http://www.allaboutindigos.com>.

Chapter Four
* * *
Indigos Are People Too!

People fail to get along because they fear each other; they fear each other because they don't know each other; they don't know each other because they have not communicated with each other. -Martin Luther King

Most of us go through life trying to find ourselves, our purpose; our *joie de vivre*. As an Indigo, there is an entirely different profundity to this. Children look to their parents and teachers for guidance; so what happens when the adults don't have a clue as to why we children are so exceptionally unique? And even worse, what happens when they try to change us and make us "normal"?

It is often said that people fear what they do not understand. And Indigos are no exception. In the old days, if you were different than what was considered *normal*, you were shunned, medicated or institutionalized. Steps were taken so that you were either docile (from medication) or actively separated from society. In the really old days, you were even killed, stoned, burned at the stake or just ostracized and forced to leave town.

Today, people point fingers and gossip about you behind your back. Or worse, they are in your face and just say rude inappropriate things right to you. If that's not enough, they publicize it and put it on the internet. It's great that we have evolved to a point of more tolerance, but really, how far have we gotten?

So here I am - an Indigo person, with abilities that are usually seen only in scary TV shows and movies. Sure we read about psychic people in books as well, but usually the books are science fiction or fantasy novels. It's not every day that we meet someone who can communicate with angels, spirit guides, dead people or animals. Or people who have the ability to work with unseen energy fields to assist others' healing.

So when others meet me, there are two frequent reactions – awe or fear. Personally, I have experienced both responses, and both are not good.

When fear is involved, people can show extreme sides of their personality; mostly ego based and judgmental. From my own experience, when people learn that I am an intuitive, and they understand all the implications of my abilities, fear can be the first reaction that is expressed. But underneath that, there is something much more intense.

Sometimes people think that I am reading their minds and they get all freaked out. Then they either shut down, where they won't talk to me, or they go into hyper defensive mode. They ask a million probing questions. I don't mind the inquisitiveness but the tonality is what gets me. It's almost like they are asserting, "You don't know what you're talking about." or "How can that be?" There is that condescending air of "You're not special enough to have those abilities; only Jesus or Saint So and So can do that." The implication is that, "You're just a stupid little kid."

But by the end of the conversation, I have already accurately told them so much about their personal life that they acquiesce and realize that regular people like me can have this ability. The unfortunate part is that they then inconvenience me at future meetings to get advice about everything going on in their life. It's not that I don't want to help them, but at some point they need to rely on their own intuition. And the extra part of this is that at some point, us Indigos need to set up personal boundaries. (See Chapter 5)

Sometimes, when other healthcare practitioners learn about what I do for a living, they get a glassed over look in their eyes and they become really quiet. If they ask me any questions about what I do, the implied reaction is usually that I am strange and that I am talking to things that I should not be talking to. It is almost like they think I am working with some creepy, spooky, dark energy. Or perhaps I have a mental disorder and am hallucinating the whole thing.

There have been others who would not ask anything but would avoid looking me in my eyes. They feared who I was, and my "supernatural powers" would immobilize them.

Even for me, the dread of being judged and isolated as the "weird intuitive" has prevented me from speaking out about my abilities.

As for the awe aspect, being put on a pedestal as being superior (different) than anyone else, doesn't feel so good either. Actually, some people are so amazed at my capabilities that for some reason, they don't think that I should even be going to school for anything, since obviously, I have all the answers at my beck and call. Just tune into the right frequencies, and you too can get the answers to all the questions on your physics exam. Now that is funny!

I am still human and I still need to learn things on this 3D plane. Information is not always given to me from other realms. As I have said before, we all have karmic issues and life lessons that need to be learned. And this is part of the reason that I am here in this lifetime. Learning mastery of this 3D existence, as well as other realms, is a main reason we all incarnate. My lessons just may be a bit different than yours.

Just as you can develop your intuitive abilities by going to a meditation school, I need to develop my abilities in this physical world. So, I still have to go to school just like everyone else. I hope you understand this concept. Being clair-anything is not a free ride. It is a special sensory ability. When people recognize this, it will be respected, instead of shunned.

******

After I became an intuitive, my mom and I still went to many different healing classes. There were two aspects that usually distinguished me from the rest of the class. The first was that I was the youngest attendant and the second was that I was an active intuitive already practicing with clients. Usually these two factors drew attention to me. There were some participants who were supportive of my accomplishments but there were plenty who actually resented me.

So here I was again being ostracized by my own spiritual community who felt that a young intuitive has not earned the right to be successful. I wouldn't mind this so much except that many asked for my reading on their problems; and when they didn't like what I told them, they immediately would say that I was wrong (even though I usually ended up right).

I do realize that their criticism of me was probably due to their own insecurities and lack of self worth, but projecting this on me is certainly not helping our cause as a spiritual community. And definitely it's not helping a young budding personage like me to feel good about myself. When I first started showing signs of psychic ability, my mom was really supportive of me. Probably because she already knew so much about the unseen forces that had helped her heal from her incurable illness.

Each of us needs to have an open mind. Look beyond the conventional cultural thinking. Greatness can be borne out of adversity. See your special child as perfect and watch how the Universe will support you in making it so.

If you get nothing else out of my story, I just want to emphasize that we are all made in the image of the Creator. If your Creator god is perfect, so are you and your child. Please do not treat Indigo Children as anything less than beautiful loving children. We are neither celebrities nor outcasts. And treating us as such will only make whatever situation we are in, worse. We need to clean up our personal environment and instill a sense of worthiness within us so that we can become more conscious and proud of whom we are.

I do not believe that Indigo Children are to be "managed" or controlled with medications. We are also not case studies to be analyzed and experimented with. Pointing out our differences as flaws is not helping our cause or the advancement of humanity. There are positive attributes in everyone. Start here and move forward. Then sit back and bask in the joy, light and love that your child is bringing into the world.

Chapter Five
* * *
Indigos Who Are Intuitive

There are only two ways to live your life. One is as though nothing is a miracle. The other is as though everything is a miracle. – Albert Einstein

As a little kid, I was always emotionally sensitive to others. Whenever someone in my family was upset I would go over to them and try to comfort them. My physical presence always seemed to help. This intuitive emotional sensitivity is one quality that seems universal with all Indigos.

Another would be my intuitive response to any parental requests and advice. My answer was always "I know." I knew it was better if I did my homework before I played, I knew that eating a second helping of ice cream was not good for me. I also knew that if I cleaned my room it would make my parents happy. Even though I knew what I should do, it does not mean I actually did it. That *knowing* can be translated into an Indigo wisdom-y attribute. That *resistance* of actually doing the things that were best for me is another Indigo trait.

Other than these Indigo characteristics, I was a normal run of the mill kid. I still got into fights with my brother, still tried hard to do well in school and still ate junk food. After I became a perceptive intuitive, my life changed a lot. I suddenly became so much more sensitive... to EVERYTHING. Before my intuitive abilities entirely developed, I had empathy for someone when they were upset. I simply wanted them to feel better. After my intuitive abilities fully developed, I felt discomfort (mental, emotional, or physical), when anyone (even if they were a stranger) was in distress. This latest capability was extremely tricky to acclimate to, since I went to a public high school (with a large class) seven hours a day. Being around hundreds of people daily, especially teenagers with hormonal surges and imbalances was quite difficult for me to manage energetically.

Clair-everything

When you have extraordinary abilities in hearing and seeing other dimensions, life here in the 3D can become tricky.

I always remember my first encounter on being an intuitive without really trying to be one. I was in the eleventh grade and it was the beginning of my math class. Everyone was getting settled into his or her assigned seat. My friend Matt was in my seat and I was in his. We got up and switched. As soon as I sat myself down in the new seat, I felt tremendous thumping pain in my head, specifically my temples. Now I should tell you, I am not someone who gets headaches, nor am I someone to comment to others if I have a headache; but for some reason I felt like it was not *my* headache. It felt like it was given to me.

I unconsciously asked Matt if he had a headache. He said he did. I asked him if the headache was in his temple area. Again, he said that was exactly where the pain was. He asked me how I knew all this about him. I told him in a matter of fact way that it was because *I* had one. He looked at me seriously for about five seconds and responded with a simple "oh".

All this happened when I wasn't even trying. When I was actually trying to be an intuitive, even more astounding things happened. It was about four months later, after I became certified in *The Reconnection* (a metaphysical healing modality).

My mom and I were in a class that spoke about healing techniques of Atlantis. The practitioner was selling jewelry and pendulums with Atlantean symbols. During the break, my mom and I were looking at the jewelry. Dr. H commented that he had bought a ring with an Atlantean symbol two years ago, but couldn't wear it since it created an allergic type reaction on his finger. His finger would itch; get red, blotchy and swollen. My mom suggested that I should try to intuitively read why this was happening. With my hands, I held Dr. H's ring and his associated finger. Instantly my mind was flooded with colorful 3D pictures of Dr. H and his life in Atlantis.

In that lifetime, he was a slow witted simpleton who was having an affair with a married woman. I saw him eavesdropping on the married woman while she was having marital relations with her husband. The woman was screaming out in apparent rapture, and he (Dr. H) misinterpreted it as if the woman was being tortured by her husband. So he ran in and killed her husband.

I went into great detail about the event, so much so, that I was grossed out by what I saw. To me it felt real. You have to remember that I was 16 years old and not exposed to this type of subject matter. When I was done relaying the story to Dr. H, Dr. H paused in silence for a moment, took a deep breath, looked into my eyes and said, "That is an absolutely incredible story. To be perfectly honest, I wouldn't believe a word of it …except that someone told me the same exact thing two years ago."

At this point, we had an audience around us; they were so blown away by the accuracy of my reading for Dr. H, that they too wanted information from me about their own issues.

As my abilities developed, I was finding it really annoying to channel information, talk to the angels, etc., through my head. When I was recalling Dr. H's past life, the images and voices felt like they were too close for comfort. At another time when I had just finished a channeling session, I felt like I was no longer myself. Rather, I was still *who* and *what* I had just finished channeling. Some might think that perhaps I was not grounded enough when I did the channeling. And this might be partially correct. However, for me, when I channeled, I would usually hold on to something that would keep me as grounded as possible.

I have managed to bypass this problem by maintaining more space between myself and whatever I am channeling. I now use my hands to bring in the information. My hands act like an antennae, connecting to the correct frequency. This technique of using my hands for channeling is wonderful, as it keeps my head clear so that I still have my own mind about me. I can still discern if the information that comes through is of *Love and Light,* and not just some random energy that is masquerading as such. This technique has come naturally to me since I practice several modalities that also involve use of my hands; such as Reiki and Therapeutic Touch. From my experience, getting the clairaudience and clairvoyance out of my head and coming through the antennae (hand), keeps it real. It is as if I am watching a stage show and I have my own special first row orchestra seat to see and hear everything. I do not have to be on the stage and emotionally or physically involved. For me, this works wonders, as I now have the best of two worlds without losing touch with either of them.

Personally, I have seen many channelers who have no sense of the 3D here-and-now reality. It is as if there has been a disconnect from the 3D realism due to the frequent other dimensional use of their brain neurons. This is my theory of why intuitive kids may become depressed, withdrawn or uncommunicative. When you can't distinguish between dimensions, there are bound to be challenges.

My suggestion is to work on groundedness and to also discern who you are communicating with. Ask them directly, "Are you of Love and Light?" If they don't answer "yes" or if they say nothing, then demand that they leave. They will.

Most importantly, show no fear. Low frequency energies feed off of fear and they will stick around unless you are adamant about their going.

Night Terrors

A night terror, also known as a *sleep terror*, is a sleep disorder that predominantly affects children, causing feelings of terror or dread, and typically occurring in the first few hours of sleep. Children who have night terrors are usually described as bolting upright with their eyes wide open, with a look of fear and panic. They will often scream or cry. Furthermore, they will usually sweat, breathe fast and have a rapid heart rate. Although it seems like children are awake during a night terror since their eyes are wide open, they will appear confused, be inconsolable, and will not always recognize others.

Night terrors should not be confused with nightmares which are basically just bad dreams. An estimated 1-8% of children have at least one night terror in their life but have no memory of the occurrence. For young Indigos, the percentage is probably much higher. My parents have mentioned often that when my brother (he is a closet Indigo) was about 9 to 10 months old, he used to have a series of reoccurring night terrors.

According to the pediatrician of that time, this can happen with kids who have a hyperactive imagination. At the time, my parents didn't know any better, so they accepted this explanation and did all they could to comfort their hysterical child. My mom said that sometimes it took over an hour to get my brother back to sleep. In retrospect, we now know that my brother was actually seeing etheric things that were quite scary to him.

I channeled in my brother's Regular Self of 9 months of age to get the real story:

I see demons; dark things that go Boo in the middle of the night. Here I am minding my own business when these dark things come into my dreams. So I wake up and they're still there in my room right above my rainbow (there was a painted rainbow on his wall). *I try to tell mom and dad* (telepathically), *but they do not hear me. I scream out loud. Mom and dad come to help me. -Michael, 9 months old*

From what I have read, night terrors typically occur in children between the ages of three to twelve years, with a peak onset in children aged three and a half years old.

Obviously, kids are having them at a much younger age (as my brother did), but it is being written off as something else, perhaps even colic.

Although I personally never had night terrors, many young Indigos who are clairvoyant or intuitively inclined, do have this issue to address, even before they can speak. It may show up as entities appearing in their room during bedtime or invisible friends during the day. Parents need to be aware that Indigo Children do not have a vivid imagination, but a very expansive visual acuity that most people dismiss as make-believe fantasy.

Friends and School

When I was in high school, I felt awkward telling anyone about my abilities. It is not as if spirituality or metaphysics were in vogue with celebrity status. It rarely came up in any conversations. And when it did, I usually had a feeling that people would be freaked out by my abilities. However, when people were in pain I knew where that pain was. It was also interesting that when I spoke up about their pain to them, *my* pain went away. It was like, "Thank you for sharing, but you can have your pain back."

Reactions to intuitive ability can be varied and I think I have experienced many of them. I remember one time in the twelfth grade in math class. My teacher had just helped me out with a calculus problem. The bell rang signifying the end of the day. My classmates were rushing towards the door. When my teacher was getting out of his seat next to me, I asked him if he was feeling alright. He gave me a phony smile and said he was fine. I asked him again if his head and neck hurt specifically. His reply was that actually he was having a fierce headache radiating from his neck. He asked me how I knew that. I told him I could feel his headache. He then asked me if I was an intuitive. I told him that I was. He did not act surprised.

Being an adult, he might have known something about intuitives. I'm sure if he pressed me for further information, he would have been okay with it. But I do think that his simple reaction is more the exception than the rule. Most seasoned teachers are programmed to act calm in front of their students.

Discretion is really important when telling people about your talents (especially if your talents are really unique). I guess teachers meet all kinds of kids, so this particular teacher just let it be. Plus, he had a headache, so I'm sure he just wanted to rush from me to get some aspirin to take care of it.

When I was away at college, I did mention to a friend who was into metaphysical studies (zen, veganism, yoga, meditation, spirituality, etc.) that I was an intuitive. He thought that it was "cool" and "awesome" and that it was a great gift to have. Honestly, he may be the only person of my own age who felt that way. Most kids my own age (and adults) are more fearful. They think I have some dark power where I can invoke ghosts to haunt them or I can read their minds. Actually I probably could, but it is not even something that interests me. It's like asking a seamstress to purposefully leave sharp needles in the clothing she makes. Sure, she could do it, but creating a beautiful dress is so much more fulfilling.

And then I moved onto acupuncture school. When one thinks of acupuncture, one would imagine people with a more open mind since this course of study mostly works with etheric meridians. What I found was that the students, who were considerably older than me, were pretty closed minded to the whole concept of intuitive healing.

The acupuncture classrooms were small and we were in tight quarters for 4 to 8 hours at a time. Being so energetically sensitive, I found this very uncomfortable. In class, I mostly sat away from other students, so that I wouldn't feel their energy. This is good to know if you are sensitive as well.

Always try to get an end seat (preferably near an open window or door), so that you are not surrounded by so many people with diverse and low frequency energies. It also helps to put up etheric walls of mirrors around you, facing outward, so that you are not picking up other people's energy.

In one of my classes, the teacher mentioned how the old masters of acupuncture had intuitive abilities that helped them accurately assess the patient and ultimately heal the patient more efficiently. The lecturer went on to say that it would be like someone seeing the aura (he should have said energy field as the aura is really outside the physical body) nowadays to figure out how the patient is doing. The teacher then asked the class if anyone could see auras. I was the only one to raise my hand. After class, a lot of students approached me to ask if I would read their aura. These are classmates who I had hardly spoken to in two years. Suddenly I was the popular kid in the class.

My conclusion is that possessing these abilities can be a real social stigma or not. It depends on the circles you travel in. Awkwardness, invariable questions and an emotionally draining situation, are some of the outcomes when you tell others about your intuitive gifts. Nowadays, for the most part I pretty much keep my ability under wraps. Being labeled as anything other than "normal" is a problem when you are trying to fit in with social situations. Yes, you should be proud of your intuitive gifts, but use discernment when sharing this information.

The Grid

When I started to perform The Reconnection™ sessions, I would see an etheric grid on the client's energy field. The grid looked like blue 3D graph paper. When the person's health was in disharmony the grid would also look disharmonious. As the patient responded well to the channeled in energy, so did their etheric grid.

As I became more heart centered, I started to notice this grid on plants and animals as well. Actually it is on everything, even those things that we consider non-living, like furniture, walls, and even food. Everything has a consciousness and it must be on a grid, albeit a different grid.

To learn more about the grid, I found myself communicating with the trees. The trees have been here for thousands of years, and through their direct connection with the Earth, they pretty much know everything.

When I was walking Celeste (my dog) in the park one day, I started to prepare to talk to her. To even try to talk to her, I had to get extremely heart centered. She told me to breathe in deeply; in through my nose and out through my mouth. As I changed my breathing, the trees started to connect to me energetically. First, it was through their branches to my branches (arms). Then the trees connected to my legs, through their legs (roots).

I started to see a holographic grid pattern overlapping the actual trees. The grid was not on one tree but connected to all the trees and grass. As I became more heart centered, I saw that the grid was connected to us as well. The quote that I have often heard my mom say, finally clicked: "We are all one."

And we are. – Diandra

Connecting to the grid is a birthright that we all possess. And for those of us who are psychic, I personally feel that it is imperative that we connect to this grid often. It keeps us grounded, provides protection, and gives us guidance on what to do in sticky situations.

It is a universal grid that connects all the psychic children, especially those with an open heart. When you are connected to the grid, you will never feel alone. There will always be other people just like you waiting to connect. It is a pure channel. Low frequencies are not allowed. This is the message from the consciousness of the grid:

We are the Children of Oz. Our matrix grid is blue and our rainbow is always present. If you haven't found us already, and you are an Indigo, we will help you to find your way here for guidance. Here is our meditation for you:

Find a relaxing place. Close your eyes and breathe deeply. Imagine rainbow light coming down through your Crown. Radiate it through your body, through your spine, torso, arms and legs. See this rainbow energy coming through your feet into the center of the Earth, grounding you. Imagine that the air you breathe is also rainbow.

You may start to feel tingly and floaty. This is a sign that you are connecting. Through your Third Eye, look for the rainbow and the blue grid. It is bright royal blue in color. You may see the children on each of the grid points. Continue to breathe deeply and radiate the rainbow through you.

Ask anything that you feel needs an answer. We will always be here to help you. Remember to connect and we are here.

I have connected many times with this grid. It is comforting and always provides positive helpful guidance. It is here for all Indigos, regardless of age. It may take a little effort to find it, but with persistence, you will.

I should mention that there are many different frequencies of grids in the Ethers. There are ones for Angels, another for Ascended Masters, another for Guides, and another for pets, etc. The Children of Oz grid is specifically for us Indigo Children. You and I are never alone. The Universe is here to support us. Just reach out and make the effort to meet it. You will not be disappointed.

Energetically Clearing Your Space

The energetic aspect of the home is very important to the well being of a sensitive Indigo.

Everything has a vibration or frequency. Just because you can't see or hear something, it doesn't mean it's not there. If you can sense that something is present in your home and it shouldn't be there, then it probably is real. And certainly, if you can hear, see, smell or feel it (invisible touches), then it is time to take action.

For those of us with no sixth sense abilities, a great example of invisible energy would be a dog whistle sound. No one would doubt that the sound is very real to the dog, even if we don't hear the sound ourselves. And for those of us with some extrasensory abilities, you usually can sense or know when something is energetically unpleasant in your home.

Honestly, the home may have much energy within it that we may not sense at all. Even those of us who have sixth sense capabilities may not sense all eerie energies. It really depends on how perceptive and sensitive you are.

Here are some basic signs on how to tell when the home needs an energetic clearing:

- Pets of your home are staying away from certain areas of your home
- Your dog is barking at something that seems like nothing is there
- Disturbed or unsettling sleep, creepy dreams
- Appliances turning themselves on and off even though no one is touching them
- Lights flashing
- Certain areas of the home have extreme temperature changes
- Getting chills, creepy crawly skin, spasms in your body (assuming that you are not sick) when you stay in certain areas of the home or speak about certain people or on certain topics
- Smelling particular smells that don't make sense in your home; like cigar smoke or favorite perfume smells from deceased loved ones
- Hearing your name called, even though no one is home or everyone who is home says it wasn't them
- Seeing spirits fully or moving shadows out of the corner of your eye
- Getting unexplained wounds/scratches, especially noticing them upon waking up in the morning
- Feeling itchy for no reason

- Intuitively feeling that something is not right in the home; people on edge, getting sick

I have had some of these occurrences happen to me. Sometimes unnatural energies are just passing through. But more often than not, these energies may end up getting comfortable in your home unless you go out of your way to get them to leave.

It can be a simple request as, *"I demand all low frequency energies that are not of Love and Light leave now. You are not welcome here. I demand that you leave now."*

If you feel chills or air moving around you, or feel any of the things on the list above, you can bet that there really is something from another dimension in your home.

At this point, I would say *"All Creator (G-d, Goddess, Ascended Masters, Angels and Archangels, Buddha, etc.) energies of Love and Light, please be with me now. Thank you for escorting this low frequency energy to wherever it needs to be for its highest path of enlightenment. Thank you."*

Usually this will do the trick. If that doesn't work, you can go on to say, *"Anyone of Love and Light who knows this entity, please be here now and escort this lost energy to wherever it needs to be for its highest path of enlightenment. Thank you."*

Sometimes a lost soul needs to recognize the being that is escorting it before it will go. Not everyone recognizes the higher frequency energies of every god/goddess. The lost soul feels a need to resonate with whoever is escorting it away, or it will not leave.

And finally you can continue to clear the space by requesting, *"Ascended beings of Love and Light, please remove all cords of attachment between me, my home, my family (you can name them individually for clarity purposes), and this energy that has been cleared. Please vacuum all the debris from this clearing and send this energy to the Light to be transmuted for the highest good of all concerned. Thank you."*

And that will usually do it. If you still feel that there is something lingering, it may be time to call in a professional space clearer for this purpose. Personally, I have done many clearings of many homes and people. At times, there can be sticky alien energies that do not move easily. Some may have to be taken in pieces due to all the cords of attachments and some have hidden layers of cronies that may be present, but not seen until you get through the layers above them. Some may have a message that they want to tell. It doesn't matter. My philosophy is if they don't belong; they have to leave. Period.

It does help if you get yourself grounded before doing this clearing, as it will keep you from losing power and falling into the fear mode. Bringing in the element of smoke and fire through the use of sage and candles can also be a benefit. Sometimes I have a CD playing with grounding sounds (dolphins, nature, singing bowls, etc.) in the background to assist in keeping the whole situation and me, more fully in my power.

Clearing space can be a very easy thing to do. A little white light, a little angel energy, a bit of sage or perhaps some high frequency sounds like Tibetan bells or whale music will usually do the trick. But sometimes more may be needed. So what do you do when some persistent low frequency energies come in and refuse to leave?

You might find this personal story useful:

My mom and I just spent 3 days out of town learning a little more about how to work with the angelic realm.

The most significant lesson I learned was not in the class. It was a real life encounter with some zombie looking lost souls that visited me in the hotel room in the middle of the night. Just for the record, this was not a run-down shabby hotel, but quite an upscale modern edifice, so I really did not expect to have this kind of issue here. But one never knows what will present itself when you are seeing into the fifth dimension.

To begin with, in the classroom lecture, the teacher emphasized the security and capability of the archangels. But in my real life encounter of needing them, this was not the case.

It was Sunday 2 a.m. and I was finding it hard to fall asleep. When I did start to feel drowsy and my eyelids started to close, I noticed zombie images materializing in front of me. I would like to mention that I did not eat anything weird that night, nor did I watch any scary shows that had anything resembling these kinds of images. Generally, when I do see dead people, they can be in 3D and in full color or black and white, or 2D in full color or black and white. I have never seen zombies before though.

As this was going on, I was thinking back about how auspicious it was that one of the teachers just told us his personal story about being on an airplane with turbulence, and when he called on the archangels to help, the turbulence stopped. The teacher then went on to say that if you need help, call on the archangels and they will assist you.

Since the images of the zombies were not going away, and I saw them with both my eyes open and closed, I called on the archangels. I asked, pleaded, begged, prayed, cajoled them for help or assistance; nothing happened.

Now I have to tell you, I am really sensitive to energies. Even when I am not actively trying to see angels or archangels, I see them. So you can guess how annoyed I was for not hearing from them or seeing them now when I really needed them. Also, I must note that usually, I can talk to the dead and get them to give me some space. Again, this was not the case. They actually got closer and the images of them got clearer. This was indicating to me they were having fun with me.

So I called upon my usual backup team. I began with Master Mikao Usui, a Japanese Buddhist who created the healing art of Reiki. Since I am a Reiki Master Teacher, and have used many of the techniques of Reiki to help with these kinds of circumstances, I thought Master Usui would be appropriate. Instead, Master Usui said that I should talk to the Egyptian Goddess Isis. Isis said to talk to Pele, the Hawaiian Goddess of fire and volcanoes. Pele very quickly showed me how to protect myself and the room. The zombies were gone immediately.

The next day, at the angel class, I asked one of the teachers why the archangels were not helpful when I needed them; his answer: "Some dead souls don't resonate with angels; it is a religious thing. Some resonate better with Buddha, Ganesh, Christ, Ascended Masters. It depends."

My brain at this moment is thinking, "So I have to feel the wrath of some dead people because the dead people do not like who I am calling in for help?" Does that sound bogus to you or is it just me? It is like saying I'm not going to help you even if you really need it because I am not the same religion as you.

The angels and archangels are non-denominational. The dead people are dead. They have no right to be able to keep me up at 2 in the morning. My point being this: just because a supposed teacher either spiritually based or otherwise says something, that does not mean it is true. My other thought is that most of the archangels have never been human, so in my opinion, they don't seem to understand human suffering; they think everything is a lesson to learn (I talked to the archangels personally after this event; they said they did not help since I needed to learn a lesson.) Are you kidding me?????

I need to also point out that a similar event has happened before. I called on the archangels and they did not assist then either. I remember that I went on strike for a while and refused to talk to them for a bit of time after this.

My main point is if one source of clearing does not work, try another. **Just remain stalwart, show no fear and try a different approach.** *Somebody up there is always looking out for us, even if it's not your first choice.* –Diandra

For those who are wondering, here is Pele's clearing that I used to remove the low frequency energies. It is worth a try if other techniques don't work:

Ground yourself. Energetically run volcano fire from the crown chakra to your feet through your core. Radiate this out through you to the space. Surround the perimeter of the space with this energy flow. Know Pele is with you and then say:

"I am guided and protected. I am full of Love and Light."

I hope these suggestions work for those who have uninvited guests in their homes. My mom often says, "If they aren't paying rent, then it's time for them to leave."

If you stay strong and in the emotion of Love (not fear), you should succeed in evicting them.

Chapter Six
* * *
Our Daily Environment

I know God will not give me anything I can't handle. I just wish that He didn't trust me so much. -Mother Teresa

There have always been frequent warnings about toxins in our environment. Some we have control over; most we don't. There is nothing I can say to assure parents that their innocent children are safe from these neuron and endocrine disrupters that are harming them. Therefore we must do all we can to protect our children, as well as ourselves.

If you add these toxins to an unhappy home life (family arguments, bullying), your sensitive Indigo can develop a major problem. So it is really important that as parents, we educate ourselves and do as much as possible to protect our children. Many of the topics that we discuss here can be applied to everyone to create improved health and harmony in the entire family.

Contaminants are found everywhere; our food, air, shelter and medicine. Unless you live in the wilderness, grow your own food and meditate daily, it is difficult to avoid them.

- **De-stress your home**

Be he a king or a peasant, he is happiest who finds peace at home. -Johann Wolfgang Von Goethe

There is a needed emotional environment for an Indigo to flourish. First there has to be people who support that Indigo. Indigos are more sensitive so they have to be treated with more awareness. This means no screaming, yelling, cursing, hitting or belittling allowed. Not at your child. Not at your spouse. Not at your neighbor.

If these distressing kinds of antics are in the presence of an Indigo, then imbalance, frustration and ultimately anger, depression or emotional and mental illness may manifest.

From our personal experiences and from helping many clients' different situations, we can honestly say that the outcome is never good, and at times seemingly irreversible.

Our theory is that an overstressed Indigo has three possible outcomes.

Outcome #1: Turning inward

When put into a stressful situation, it is not unusual for anyone to retreat. It's a bit more obvious for an Indigo. The Indigo may go silent, stay in a corner or quiet space and not talk to anyone. Go inward where it's safe. Most Indigos are communicating telepathically anyway, so why would they want to communicate with a world that's so stressful.

They might learn that only a certain person in the household is the troublemaker and eventually stop talking to that one person. The result will be a closed down heart and throat chakra. Unfortunately, this could manifest as thyroid issues, lung or cardiac conditions. They might even be diagnosed with an emotional disorder such as autism or Aspergers syndrome.

They might never feel safe to talk, or share their ideas. Communication challenges later in life are inevitable. When the heart chakra closes down they might find it hard to trust others or have a difficult time maintaining a true deep loving relationship with anyone. Unresolved repressed anger is usually the outcome.

Outcome #2: Acting out

Then there is the other Indigo personality who is very headstrong. So when they are stressed out, they scream or fight back. Your kid could be a perfect angel at home but constantly get into fights and talk back to teachers at school. Or she could be a handful at home and you have no idea why the teachers think she's a perfect treasure in the classroom. So it's hard to really know how this will play out.

Either way, it's not good since this may eventually lead them to snap. Extreme violence, pulling a gun or knife may become the outcome. And we have seen this too often occurring in schools across the country. 'Going postal' is not just for the USPS workers. Anyone with repressed anger or deep emotions is a potential explosion waiting to happen.

The consequences could be a lot of anger, hate, self-serving tendencies, a superiority complex, guilt, and possible violence in the future.

Outcome #3: Losing control of intuitive abilities

A very unfortunate result for Indigos, who are intuitive, is to have their abilities go haywire. When the walls, plants and furniture start talking to them, and won't be quiet, then you know there is a situation that needs immediate attention. Hearing voices and not being able to control this gift is definitely bordering on a diagnosable psychosis. A frightened, unstable person needing medicines to appear functionally normal in our 3D world is not what we want our kids to grow into.

Another plausible outcome to losing control is being afraid of one's own intuitive abilities. This could lead to a whole host of other issues. If angels, dead people or unfriendly spirits show up, fear may be the first reaction. This will either keep the Indigo anxious or convince them to turn off their abilities. Neither one is a good result.

No family is perfect, mine included. I remember when my family had fights; I could hear the dog crying out to me, the plants pleading and the walls asking for peace. I wanted the yelling to stop, the walls to be quiet. I would take Celeste and leave; until things would quiet down. Thankfully, I have since managed to control these etheric voices. -Diandra

So what do we do to prevent all this? Well, we have a pretty hefty list of what we have done and we have included all the basic secrets that we know below. Sure there are plenty more, but our suggestions are easily applied by anyone without relying on outside involvement.

And if you are asking why you should do this, the answer is simple: Indigos are sensitive to EVERYTHING. So if something in your environment creates an adverse reaction on a regular non-sensitive person like you, then the effect on an Indigo will be much more intense. So intense that it may create weird physical, mental and emotional symptoms that conventional medicine has no cure for. Your child will just become another statistic and will be offered a host of drugs to keep them asymptomatic and silent.

The important thing to keep in mind is that we are all assaulted by hundreds if not thousands of toxic materials from our environment every day. Most are insidious, hidden in food, medicines, air, and invisible sound waves. We can't hide ourselves in a plastic bubble all day and night, but we can take control and start removing the ones that are obvious.

- **Detoxify Your Home**

The most important work you and I will ever do will be within the walls of our own homes. –Harold B. King, US Mormon clergyman

Sick building syndrome is not just for people who work in poorly ventilated office buildings. According to the World Health Organization, up to 30% of new and remodeled buildings worldwide may be linked to this syndrome. But it is also present in older buildings as well.

It usually comes down to flaws in heating, ventilation or air conditioning. Other contributing factors include the outgassing of volatile organic compounds (VOC) like formaldehyde and plastics from new construction materials (new carpeting is really bad), mold or inordinate amounts of dust, dirt and animal hairs.

Since moving from your home may be impossible, here is a checklist of what you can do to lessen the toxicity in your home:

- Keep your house as clean as possible. Dust and vacuum daily. Change the bed linens at least twice a week. Remove all carpeting. Not only does carpeting outgas, it also collects tons of dirt in the microfibers that you are breathing in constantly. Adverse health effects suffered by carpet installers are a clear-cut way to see the hazards of this product. Most documented are neurological problems and higher rates of cancer. If you must have carpet, make sure that it is as natural as possible.

- Use natural cleaners. Replace chemical cleaners with essential oils, baking soda and vinegar. Tea tree oil is especially effective at removing mold and mildew.

Baking soda acts as an abrasive to remove stains and residue from glass, ceramic and stainless steel. You can add a few drops of water to make a paste to clean the stove, sink, tub or toilet. White vinegar is excellent as a window and mirror cleaner. Add your favorite essential oil if you want a pleasant smell.

Recipe for an easy non-toxic all purpose cleaner: 1 cup white vinegar, 5 drops tea tree oil, 5 drops lavender oil, ½ cup water. Mix in a labeled spray bottle. That's it. It is great to use on counters, and stove tops. It is not meant for porous surfaces such as wood. It costs pennies to make and even the most sensitive person will have virtually no perceptible reaction. You can use less water to make it stronger.

As a side note to this, you should avoid all artificially fragranced products: air fresheners, household cleaners, detergents. Unscented may very well be a highly processed product. It takes a lot of chemicals to mask a smell, so fragrance-free may be toxic chemical-full. Fluffer sheets used in the dryer can be more toxic than your detergent. Use the silicone dryer balls instead. Plus it is much more cost effective, as they have an infinite reusable lifespan. As always, read ingredient lists carefully to make sure your product is as natural as possible.

- Remove plastic from your eating arsenal. If you have any plastic dishes or cups, throw them out. Bis phenyl

A (BPA) is a known xenoestrogen and will affect the hormone balance of your body. Besides its known carcinogenic effect, it will also create imbalance within your endocrine system and ultimately affect mental and physical development. Leaking of bis phenyl A into your water from plastic bottles has already been documented. And the longer the water has been in the bottle, the more BPA you will be ingesting.

Xenoestrogen is one of the most troubling types of endocrine disruptors. It will mimic estrogen and attach to the body's estrogen-receptor sites; in both sexes (notice men are developing breast overgrowth). These xenoestrogens interfere with hormonal signaling and are believed to cause an increased risk of hormonal imbalances contributing to breast, prostate, and reproductive cancers; reduced fertility; early puberty in children; menstrual irregularities; endometriosis; numerous cysts and other disorders.

An interesting occurrence just happened with our dog Celeste. She has pretty much always eaten from stainless steel bowls. But about 6 months ago, we started serving her home cooked food from the plastic container that it was stored in, in the refrigerator. She developed a little growth on her lip. The veterinarian said that Celeste probably bit herself and a little fibroma formed. Then about 3 weeks ago, part of her nose started changing color from black to pinkish white. This time we went online to see if we could find the answers ourselves. Not wanting to buy into the gloom and doom of my dog being old (she's 3) or has a weird skin condition or blame it on the weather (hard to believe but seasonal change will cause this shift), we looked further. There was something we found about chemicals in plastic dishes possibly creating the color change. We figured this would be a simple thing to correct. We immediately changed all her serving bowls back to stainless or ceramic. Guess what? In three days, not only was her nose changing back to normal color but that growth on her lip was also disappearing. One week later, there was no trace of any dis-ease on her nose or lip. My beautiful healthy puppy had her baby face back.

Thank you Celeste for that personal real live lesson on the dangers of plastics in our environment. The thing to realize is that Celeste is a 12 pound dog. The effects on her were visually seen. If you are a 50 or 150 pound person, the effects will not be so obvious. However, you should know that theses toxins are accumulating in your body, and affecting every part of you- skin, hair, brain, and especially your hormone systems that control everything. Plastics have chemicals that will act like hormones and this will throw your whole body out of whack.

Celeste has a very clean healthy diet, so her body immediately threw the toxins to the skin surface in an attempt to remove them. I doubt that us humans will be that lucky. It will take a bit more effort than that.

- Do not use the microwave. Microwave ovens are radiation ovens. When you say it like that, the reality of this machine is clear. The microwave radiation distorts the molecular structure of the foods; it destroys much of the nutrients and causes many problems with the immune system. If you value your health, take the extra couple of minutes to heat the food up the right way.

- Limit cell phone use. Cell phones expose us to a form of electromagnetic radiation (EMF) energy. Scientists have suspected that this radiation might increase the risk of brain cell damage leading to tumors, and in 1995 they found this to be the case in rats. An analysis of the most rigorous studies found convincing evidence linking the use of handheld phones to brain tumors, especially in users of a decade or longer. Regardless of brain tumors, we personally know of people who feel physically ill when using the cell phone. It affects brainwaves. That's enough information for me. Use it sparingly and stick to the land line (NOT cordless) as much as possible. Buy an EMF protector and install it on your cell phone.

- Limit computer use. Besides the obvious eye and wrist strain, there is a generating of EMFs. Nobody would sit at a desk under high voltage power lines. Yet we will happily sit a foot away from a computer screen, with a computer and printer on the desk next to us, and perhaps even a power supply near our feet. The old box-shaped cathode-ray tube (CRT) computer monitors generally have quite high levels of radiation. Best to invest in a flat screen monitor. And of course EMF protectors are essential.

- Limit television watching or better yet, remove it completely from the home. Research shows that your brain literally shifts into a passive state when you're watching television. Experiencing "brain fog" is not uncommon. Your alpha brain waves increase after television exposure. Alpha waves are commonly associated with a relaxed meditative state as well as brain states associated with suggestibility. You can achieve a good alpha state through meditation – and that can be an active process producing insight and calm. Too much time spent in the low alpha wave state caused by TV can cause unfocussed daydreaming and inability to concentrate. Researchers have said that watching television is similar to staring at a blank wall or sitting in a dark room for several hours.

  Aside from this induced state of brain wave altering, most shows are advertisement driven with subliminal messages. And because of this suggestibility state that you are already in, you are more likely to watch shows that are violent or inappropriate for a healthy growing mind. In our home, we have gone many years with limited or no TV, and I think we turned out alright. Anything that you really want to see can easily be found through the internet.

- Remove electronics from the bedroom, especially TV, computers, radio alarm clocks. Again they release a continual dose of EMFs. And if they must be present, then they should be as far away from your head as possible when sleeping and as close to the floor as possible.

- Remove your shoes before coming into your home. Tracking in dirt and germs from outside into the home should be avoided.

- Discard all aluminum or Teflon based cookware. Aluminum will leach into your food. It is a known neurotoxin, causing brain degeneration. Teflon or stick free cookware will eventually chip and enter your food. Better to use high quality stainless steel, cast iron or titanium.

- Do not use aluminum or plastic wrap on foods. And definitely do not microwave anything in or covered with plastic. We usually wrap foods in wax paper first and then outside wrap this with foil or plastic wrap.

- Invest in an air purifier and negative ionizer to eliminate air borne toxins – mold spores, dust, cigarette smoke, pet hair, hydrocarbon toxins and remnants of chemtrails from outside that we may be carrying into our homes.

- Remove fluoride from your intake. This includes toothpastes, mouthwashes, fluoride rinses and municipal drinking water.

The government first began encouraging municipal water systems to add fluoride in the early 1950s. Since then, fluoride has been put in toothpaste and mouthwash. It is also in a lot of municipal tap waters, bottled waters, and all drinks and foods made from them, including soda, reconstituted juices and baked goods. Additionally, some children may even be prescribed fluoride supplements.

Since 1962, the fluoridated water standard has been in a range of 0.7 parts per million for warmer climates where people drink more water, to 1.2 parts per million in cooler regions. To add insult to injury, 1% – 5% of the population is intolerant to fluoride. These people do not experience an allergic reaction (although that is what the government calls it) but a poisoning reaction. Sodium fluoride has been used for decades as a rat poison and insecticide.

As a result there has been a fluoride overdosing. The most obvious marker for this is in the increase in discoloration of our children's teeth. The less obvious marker is the acknowledged deterioration of our children's brain function. It has already been documented that sodium fluoride is a neurotoxin. It affects the endocrine system, causes bone fluorosis, cancer and brain damage. Just look at a tube of toothpaste and read the warning.

> **WARNING: Keep out of the reach of children under 6 years of age.** If you accidentally swallow more than used for brushing, get medical help or contact a Poison Control Center right away.

I think this label pretty much puts a lid on the topic. No more to say other than, "Why would anyone put this stuff in their mouth?" Goodness knows that if it's in your mouth, you are going to swallow some of it. It's just not possible not to.

This reminds me to mention that you should purposely request *no fluoride treatments* for your children at their dental visits. Just because it comes highly recommended and insurance companies will pay for it, that doesn't mean it's good for you. Even if you receive it for free from your dental insurance carrier, that doesn't make this poison any less toxic. As a practicing dentist for many decades, I have heard several stories of young children dying from acute fluoride overdose in the dental office. Do not let you or your child become a statistic.

Now, what do you do if it's in the municipal tap water, and all the drinks and foods made from it? It's pretty scary when you start thinking about how much fluoride you are really taking in. It is important to note that fluoride safety has never been approved by the FDA. *Fluoride ingestion does not reduce tooth decay.* Its predominant anti-caries effect is topical, not systemic. And certainly there are safer ways to prevent cavities than the use of fluoride. (How about cutting down the frequency of sugary sticky foods? Or rinsing your mouth with plain water after you eat them?).

The bottom line is that the water supply should not be used as a drug delivery system to individuals without regard to age, weight, health, need, and informed consent. *Fluoride is the only water additive intended to treat people and not the water.* It may not be long before the cities routinely start adding other chemicals to treat people. There has already been talk of adding trace amounts of Lithium to our water to suppress bipolar, manic depressant disorder and suicide.

- Invest in a water purifier. City water is loaded with chemicals to make it potable. We have a double carbon and alumina filter installed under our sink. You may need a plumber to install it, but it is definitely worth the expense. Not only does the water taste cleaner, but you are actually getting quality water that will help your body detoxify properly, instead of poisoning it even more.

Bottled spring water is not the answer, as this will only give you toxins from the plastic containers. Our sensitive children (and us) are precious. It is much easier to actively work at omitting these toxins from our life instead of waiting to see if we get sick from them. By the time we notice the effect upon us, there will be so many adverse and diverse symptoms that it may be almost impossible to regain our health. It is not just an issue of removing toxins from our bodies but also an issue of rebuilding our bodies from that damaged point. It takes years to get sick, and it will probably take just as long to regain health.

Other options beside the carbon and alumina filters would include installing a reverse osmosis filter or a water distiller to remove everything that's not water. You might have to add some mineral salts back to the water so that you do not become mineral deficient. Most pitcher water filters are carbon filters. They are better than nothing but they will not remove fluoride (a confirmed pituitary, pineal and thyroid gland toxin).

As a side note, boiling water does not remove toxins. It will just kill living organisms (bacteria, parasites, mold, etc.) that may be present. Chemical toxins will still be present. Also, for those energetically aware, the life force of the water will be lowered considerably. So if you are going to make any hot beverage, best to heat the water to right below the boiling temperature.

- Consider having your home tested for mold, radon and lead.

- Add plants to your home. Not only will they help keep you grounded energetically, they will also clean the air you breathe. Some easily found varieties such as spider plant, snake plant, English ivy and Boston fern are known to filter harmful chemicals. Make sure that the plants you bring into your home are not poisonous to your pets.

- Clean out all air ducts and vents regularly. Investigate the use of furnace filters. Be sure that a carbon monoxide detector is up in your home so that you are not breathing this insidious noxious odorless gas.

- Open windows regularly. Indoor air pollution is always more dangerous than outdoor air pollution, even in busy industrialized cities.

By integrating just one of these techniques into your life and maintaining it, your life will change for the better dramatically. The ability to think clearer and sleep better should be obvious within a few weeks, if not sooner. Prevention is worth more than a pound of cure. Get started today.

- **Detoxify You**

The best way to detoxify is to stop putting toxic things into your body and let it depend upon its own mechanisms. – Dr. Andrew Weil

Many of the toxins that you have in your body can be contributing to your being labeled with a dis-order. And most of these toxins, you are probably not even be aware of.

- **Have yourself tested for heavy metals.**

Heavy metal toxicity in today's society is rampant. As a practicing dentist for 30 years, and as a holistic educator, I can honestly say that heavy metals are probably the number one contributor to chronic neurological health diseases on the physical and mental planes. This includes but is not limited to Autism, Alzheimer's, Parkinson's and Multiple Sclerosis.

Mercury poisoning has been implicated in a host of chronic symptoms of dis-ease, so it might be a good eye opener to have a look at this website: http://www.mercurypoisoned.com/symptoms.html to see if any of the mercury toxicity symptoms resonate with you.

You may be wondering how you or your Indigo child could possibly have gotten into this situation. It is very easy when you understand that mercury is present in many products that we are exposed to routinely.

You remember all those tuna fish sandwiches you ate as a kid?–toxic mercury (environmental). Or how about the 22 or so vaccines that you were exposed to in the first 6 years of your life? - toxic mercury (preservative). Or the shiny silver fillings in your mouth? - toxic mercury.

And if you yourself don't have those silver mercury fillings, how about your mother who carried you for 9 months in utero. Mercury does pass through the placental barrier. That would certainly be enough to get your system exposed to a high loading dose of mercury. And as you grew up, and made your regular checkups for immunizations, your exposure only increased, augmenting the toxic load. The cumulative amount of mercury being given to children in the average number of vaccines by age 6, would be an amount equivalent to 187 times the EPA daily exposure limit!!!!

And knowing now what you didn't know before you read this, you need to take action. If you are an Indigo Child or the parent of an Indigo Child, and you have been diagnosed with a physical or mental disorder, or if you just don't feel right most of the time, I highly recommend that you be tested for heavy metal toxicity. It is a simple non-invasive urine test that is easily done at any competent physician's office.

And what do you do now? Now that you have been labeled with an "incurable" illness? Now that you need to be medicated for life to be "normal"?

THERE IS NO ILLNESS CAUSED BY A DEFICIENCY OF ANY DRUG.

Yes, that needs repeating.

THERE IS NO ILLNESS CAUSED BY A DEFICIENCY OF ANY DRUG.

When you realize this and truly believe it, you can begin to heal. You are perfection already. You are only out of balance. If you shift to this new paradigm of thinking, the healing will begin.

So how do heavy metals affect our young sensitive children? Usually through a diagnosis that says your child is not "normal". Diagnoses such as Autism, Asperger's, ADD, ADHD, Learning disabled, Depression, Bipolar disorder, PDD-NOS, Anxiety and Tremors are the most common.

The vast neurological symptoms that occur in children exposed to mercury are: decreased eye contact, repeating certain actions over and over again, not responding to their name, not looking at an object that is being pointed at by another, poor concentration or attention and sensitivity to sensory stimulation.

Common language or speech symptoms of mercury poisoning: loss of speech, delayed speech, decreased understanding and articulating words, remembering only certain words. Also common are social problems such as withdrawal, being irritated, aggressive behavior, mood swings, night terrors and other sleep problems. In addition, other symptoms include auto-immune disorders such as multiple sclerosis, juvenile diabetes, asthma, chronic ear infections, and decreased immunity.

Of course, it must be recognized that heavy metal toxicity is not the only cause of all of these disorders. However, it can be said that mercury may be an original trigger and can set off all of these syndromes. Therefore, if these symptoms are present, it is logical to check for the presence of mercury and all heavy metals. And we should bear in mind that the toxic load of heavy metals is cumulative. So that beautiful healthy young child may be a very different person later in their childhood due to the accumulation of toxins throughout the years.

Today's children are not like you and me. They are physically more sensitive to the environment than we were as children. And when their physical self is out of balance, then their mental and emotional fields will follow. They are born with a sixth sense that can easily get turned off or overloaded, and this will then manifest in so many diverse symptoms.

So if you are an Indigo that is out of balance, now would be the ideal time to rule out heavy metal toxicity as the culprit for your challenges. Do the right thing. Get the simple 24 hour urine Heavy Metal Toxicity test and learn if this is the cause of your health challenges. - Idelle

As an afterthought, there are many physicians who don't have a clue about this particular 24 hour urine Heavy Metal Toxicity test. If your doctor is not familiar with it or not willing to do this kind of heavy metal test, it may be time to find a new physician. Information is all over the internet. You would have to be a closed minded physician to belittle a heavy metal toxicity test and dismiss it as inconsequential. A simple blood test or hair analysis may be helpful but will not be conclusive enough to accurately evaluate heavy metals in your system.

- **Have yourself tested for hormone imbalance.**

It is not unusual for an imbalance in hormone levels to affect how we think and behave. Heavy metals, fluoride and xenoestrogens (from pesticides, preservatives and plastics) will affect every endocrine gland in your body. The endocrine glands are the ductless glands that are responsible for secreting hormones directly into the bloodstream. The most obvious endocrine glands affected in Indigos are the pituitary, pineal and thyroid. Other endocrine imbalances of the pancreas (type 1 diabetes is on the rise in children), the ovaries and testes (early puberty and fertility problems later in life) and the adrenals (exhaustion), actually can apply to all of us, not expressly Indigos.

The pituitary is the master gland of the body. If it is imbalanced, all the other glands will follow. Your genetics and environment will determine which other glands get the brunt of the imbalance. Directly, it will affect your growth hormones.

The pineal gland sits right behind the Third Eye area (between your two eyes and slightly up on the forehead) in your brain. For centuries the pineal was thought to be vestigial with no function at all. We now know that it has a great impact on the sleep-wake cycle due to its production of melatonin. If you have any intuitive sixth sense capabilities, it is usually through the health of your pineal gland. Fluoride will shut it down very quickly.

The thyroid gland controls how quickly the body uses energy, makes proteins, and the sensitivity of the body to other hormones. It has already been documented that heavy metals, especially mercury will cause hypothyroidism. An underactive thyroid will affect all metabolism functions. Make sure that any thyroid test is comprehensive as most routine blood tests only check the TSH level. T4 must also be evaluated to get an accurate assessment.

- **Eat healthy foods.**

Everyone knows the simple adage: *You are what you eat.*

And for those of us who are very sensitive, these words resonate on an entire other level. You cannot eat junk food and expect to feel different than "junky". Some of us can live on fast food and be okay, while others will have intense physical and even psychological reactions to the food we eat.

We have discussed the energy quality of the food affecting your health. Obviously, a meal made with love tastes a lot better than food made with anger. Remember when you went to family Thanksgiving dinners and everybody brought something to the meal. It always tasted better and emotionally felt better than even the most delicious luxurious food from take-out. There is a lot to be said for "Grandma's cooking", even if it was the most simple boring dish around. It was always made with love and you could taste it!

Touching on the food topic, it also matters the intention that goes into the food. During the first semester of my freshman year of college, I only ate the cafeteria food.

The problem was that the food had been emotionally and etherically charged with the staff of sickly workers. Most of the cafeteria people had a smoker's cough and a raspy voice. Actually, when they coughed, they sounded like they were going to choke up a lung. I could visually see the cigarette packs stuffed into their clothes (shirt sleeve or pants pocket) when they cooked and served the food.

So, guess what happened after I ate a meal? I found it was hard to breathe, my lips would swell and I felt extremely depressed. The symptoms would start soon after I ate their food. I found these side effects extremely distracting and scary. I was in my first semester of college and under a good amount of stress; heavy school load of science classes, bad roommate situation, five plus hours away from home. The food situation was not helping.

I was not intentionally trying to be an intuitive at college, so the fact that I was getting such harsh physical reactions from the food was making me really hate myself for being so sensitive, which I should have really been proud of since this sixth sense ability is a gift and should not be a hardship.

I found that I was not being true to myself (hating my gift), and feeling constantly sick; all because my dim-witted college hired low frequency people who were substandard in preparing and serving food with their limited mentality. Sure, I wasn't getting food poisoning or salmonella, but its effect was pretty similar.

After I turned my back on the cafeteria ladies, I turned to the stir-fry station. This was limited to one guy with a wok, and some vegetables, soy sauce and white rice. I thought it would be simple food, no complications. Also, the people that made and handled the food at the stir-fry station were always students from the college who were there from the work-study program. My thinking was that the students would be younger, healthier and happier than the cigarette packing cafeteria workers. Unfortunately, I was wrong. One of the guys would consistently complain about his status with his girlfriend. First they were fighting, then they broke up and then they were dating again. You get the picture. So, guess how I would feel after each meal served from this guy? My emotions were everywhere; depressed, anxious, elated and sad. Again, this was all in my first semester. I learned my lesson, and stopped eating cafeteria food and had to buy my own. - Diandra

Always monitor how your Indigo's body reacts to foods. Even infants and toddlers will give you clues.

When I was a baby, and I went from mom's milk to cow's milk, my body rejected the food. According to my dad I was diagnosed with colic and I would cry a lot. Colic is when you have an upset stomach, gas, and stomach pain. Then I got switched to soy milk. I still had colic with this beverage too. When I got switched to goat's milk, the colic was gone. I guess my body knew what was right for me. Whenever I drank cow's milk or ate a cow cheese product occasionally between the age of five and thirteen, my stomach would hurt and my sinuses got clogged. Not only did I stop having cow's milk because of my body's symptoms, but also because I learned that many hormones and antibiotics are given to the cow and then end up in us.

By that time I had started my menstrual cycle and learned that the hormones from the cow products would mess with my hormones and therefore my period, I stopped. After that, my period improved. The alternatives that I used were and still are rice milk, almond milk, hemp milk, and goat milk. For cow cheese alternatives there is goat cheese, and almond cheese.

And don't always go by allergy testing, since mine were pretty much inaccurate. When I got allergy tested during those years, I was not officially diagnosed as allergic to milk or soy, just dust. My point being, as an Indigo, my body is really sensitive to what I eat and I need to listen to how it responds to whatever I ingest.

From my own experience, reading these foods energetically and from my clients' experience, I have found that gluten products slow down the body, can make a person feel depressed, and feel like they cannot think. I stay away from gluten products as much as possible; luckily there are a lot of gluten free products. If there is a need to bake, which I often do, I have used millet flour, coconut flour, arrowroot flour, brown rice flour, buckwheat flour, chickpea flour or garbanzo flour instead of wheat flour. Now I can make desserts and have my healthy junk food, just like everybody else. -Diandra

Healthy food is an important key for Indigo vigor. A lot of Indigos have a tendency to think that they know what is best for them. Translation: Indigos can have a stubborn streak. So they might carry on for the sugar, soda, chips and white bread that their friends have, especially for lunch at school. Please do not give into their bargaining, begging and groveling. It will often end badly. Especially stay away from the sugar products; fake sugars are the worst. Natural sugars are fine, like the ones found in fruit, agave (may be processed so be careful), lucuma, molasses, cane juice, coconut palm sugar, xylitol, grade B maple syrup, and raw honey. Not only does processed sugar get the body hyper, but it also messes with sensitive minds, creating all kinds of learning and behavior challenges.

Finally, we need to show gratitude for our food. Give thanks for the plant that grew your veggies, for the animal that created that burger. Say a short blessing or thankful words before you chow down. And most importantly, try to eat organic and local farmers' foods as much as possible. An apple fresh off the tree yesterday is going to have more nutrition and taste better than the apple from 3000 miles and a week's truck ride away.

- **Avoid processed foods**

I usually tell clients "If it comes in a package with a list of ingredients that you can't pronounce, don't eat it!" Nobody wants to eat poisons, even if they taste good. If you can't find tasty real foods in the supermarket, now would be a good time to check out your local health food store to see what a better choice would be. Look for raw or whole food clubs in your area. Find a like minded friend and create your own club. You can be **that** person who creates *the healthy food cooking club* in your neighborhood. If you don't know what to cook, learn! Have a look at the many *YouTube* videos that show you exactly how to make real food, and try it. There is actually no excuse for being ignorant to the healthy food revolution, as there are more and more health minded cooking schools now open in many big cities.

Many processed foods have hidden sugars in them. Some can be obvious but many are not. Replace chemicalized food with real food. Simple condiments like table salt have sugar added to make it taste better. If you read the ingredient list on Ketchup, don't be surprised to find that tomatoes are not the first ingredient. We all need to be conscious of what we are putting in our bodies. Yummy tasting additives are not nourishing food. They are there as inexpensive fillers and prolongers of product shelf life. They will not nourish your body, mind or spirit. Quite contrary, they will deplete your health and create imbalance and disease. Our good health depends on us making healthy food choices.

- **Avoid artificial sugars, fats, colors and flavors.**

Buying sugar free or fat free foods is not a solution when chemicals are added to replace the missing flavors and textures. If anything, it has already been proven that these artificially flavored foods actually make us hungrier. And the reason is simple: Your body will continue to crave real nutrition from real food. If you are only fed artificial food with artificial "enriched" vitamins added, you will continue to be hungry until fed the nutrients that your body needs and wants.

Besides these artificial ingredients providing no natural nourishment, they are toxic chemicals that are poisoning you, slowly over time.

Sodium saccharine (Sweet-N-Low) was the first artificial sweetener developed. It was accidentally created in 1879 by a researcher at Johns Hopkins University in Baltimore, when he noticed that a derivative of coal tar he accidentally spilled on his hand tasted sweet. Now more than 125 years later, saccharin is joined by a growing list of artificial sweeteners with varying chemical structures and uses including acesulfame potassium; aspartame (NutraSweet or Equal); sucralose (Splenda), and D-Tagatose (Sugaree). And there's a whole host of new ones on the horizon.

Trans fatty acids (margarine or shortening) or fat substitutes (Simplesse, Oatrim, Olestra), and products fortified by plant based ester compounds are found in most processed foods. Next time you reach for coffee creamer, margarine, crackers, bread, or even your favorite brand of potato chips, flip over the bag and take a look at the ingredients--if you see hydrogenated or partially hydrogenated oil of any type, you're eating a trans fatty acid. The consequences include increased occurrence of heart disease, sexual dysfunction, weakened immune system, cancer, atherosclerosis, diabetes, intestinal problems, and obesity.

It seems that so much food on our supermarket shelves is marketed specifically to children. That is extremely dangerous. Kids are attracted to labels that have cartoon characters on them. Kids are also attracted to bright, colorful foods. The food companies know this, and that is why a good chunk of foods that are made specifically for children are loaded with artificial food dyes.

Studies have shown that artificial food colors and flavors are associated with the following conditions: allergies, asthma, behavioral issues, hyperactivity, and ADHD, decreased cognitive function, lowered IQ, cancer and brain tumors.

I don't know about you, but those are all things I hope I can help my child avoid. So what can we do? Educate ourselves. Here's a look at the specific food dyes you will find in common foods throughout and their known effects:

- *Yellow #5*: hyperactivity, eczema/hives, aggressive/violent behavior, asthma, irritability, sleep disturbances/insomnia, increased susceptibility to infection
- *Yellow #6*: hyperactivity, eczema/hives, asthma,
- *Red #40:* hyperactivity
- *Red #3:* Tumors, neurochemical and behavioral effects

Artificial flavors are linked to allergic and behavioral reactions, yet these ingredients are not required to be listed in detail as they're *generally recognized as safe* (GRAS) by the FDA.

MSG (monosodium glutamate) is a popular flavor enhancer. Found to cause brain damage in laboratory mice, it has been banned from use in baby foods, but is still used in many other foods, processed or from restaurants. It causes common allergic and behavioral reactions including headaches, dizziness, chest pains, depression, and mood swings, and is also a possible neurotoxin.

What many people don't know is that more than 40 different ingredients contain the chemical in monosodium glutamate (processed free glutamic acid) that causes these reactions. The most common ingredients that form this toxic free glutamic acid include: corn starch, corn syrup, modified food starch, dextrose, rice syrup, malt extract, soy sauce, yeast extract, *anything* hydrolyzed, *anything* hydrolyzed protein, *anything* flavors or *anything* flavoring, seasonings, carrageenan, bouillon, broth, stock, maltodextrin, citric acid.

That has got to affect the majority of any packaged food that comes in a can or box at the supermarket. What often fooled me was the term *natural flavorings*, thinking it was a healthy ingredient. Then I found out that this is a euphemism for MSG or aspartame.

PLEASE READ INGREDIENTS BEFORE BUYING!!!

- **Remove heavy metals and plastics (xenoestrogens) from your diet.**

Whether you have been diagnosed with heavy metal toxicity or not, I recommend the following protocol to keep heavy metal accumulation to a minimum. Once you realize that heavy metals are in almost everything, you will also realize that you need to be proactive in detoxing and not accumulating more of it.

You will probably need to work with a health professional on this, as it can become tricky and quite uncomfortable. Even if you have never had a silver mercury filling placed in your teeth, you should still be evaluated to rule out the heavy metal factor contributing to your imbalance. Heavy metals are unknowingly passed to our children in utero (does mom or dad have any mercury fillings or root canals?), from food (especially high mercury fish and foodstuff treated with pesticides, antibiotics and hormones), paints, and vaccines.

1. If you have any silver mercury fillings in your teeth, have them replaced. Make sure to work with a qualified holistic dentist who knows the proper protection protocol when your silver mercury fillings are drilled out. Otherwise you may expose yourself to massive amounts of toxic mercury vapor causing a tremendous exposure and dire consequences. You can find information at this website: http://iaomt.org/. I would still ask questions of the particular practitioner that you are considering to make sure they are doing the right thing for your protection.

   Also, reconsider the use of vaccines. Many have mercury (thimerosol) and aluminum added.

2. Integrate chlorophyll rich drinks into your diet. Green juices are made from green superfoods- foods like barley grass, spirulina and other chlorophyll rich foods. These superfoods are packed with the vitamins and minerals that you need for detoxifying and rebuilding your immune system.

Chlorophyll from green foods supports intestinal and liver health, improves oxygen delivery by the blood, and supports elimination of certain toxins and heavy metals. It may inhibit absorption of environmental pollutants like dioxin and also help your body excrete many toxins quicker. The high antioxidant level can slow aging by combating free radical damage. It has even been shown to repair DNA! Chlorophyll also enhances oxygen transport in your body and is a top nutrient for balancing your body's pH by helping to reduce acidity. And maintaining a good body pH is so important in fighting off infections and inflammation. Low-grade acidosis may not only contribute to fatigue but other health concerns as well, including kidney stones and lower growth hormone levels, which lead to more body fat and loss of lean muscle mass.

Green juices are easily made from juicing organic vegetables or by adding any liquid to a dehydrated green juice powder. There are plenty of different brands of green juice powder at the health food store. So read the labels to find one that you feel is best for you with no allergenic additives. The powders are easy to work with as they can be added to juice, smoothies or protein drinks, which makes it fairly palatable and simple to use.

It is important to keep in mind that the health benefits of juicing are different than those received from eating green vegetables. Juice nutrients are much more easily absorbed, tolerated and utilized by the cells of your body than eating the whole vegetable with fiber. Both are healthful but juicing is so much more nutrient dense for the purposes of detoxing and rebuilding.

3. Ingest foods rich in phytoestrogens. They are found in flax seeds, sprouted beans, some fruits and vegetables. Phytoestrogens bind to the estrogen sites preventing the xenoestrogens from being bound. Do avoid soy products (tofu, soy milk, etc.) as there is much controversy on its side effects from over consumption.

4. Eat tons of cruciferous vegetables. (Preferably raw, fermented or lightly steamed). This would include cabbage, broccoli, brussel sprouts, and kale. They are rich in indole-3-carbinole. This converts to di-indolyl-methane (DIM). DIM then induces certain enzymes in the liver to block the production of toxic estrogens and improves the production of the beneficial forms. If you have a hypothyroid condition, you should consult a qualified practitioner for guidance, since

overconsumption of raw cruciferous foods may exacerbate an underactive thyroid.

5. Avoid caffeine as some studies show that it can boost estrogen levels. It is found in many foods: coffee, tea, chocolate, most sodas and even some analgesics. So please read labels carefully.

6. Avoid foods that have been treated with hormones or pesticides. These are both xenoestrogens. Eat organic as much as possible.

7. Avoid the excessive use of lavender essential oil. It has been implicated as a xenoestrogen.

- **Use natural personal care products.**

There are thousands of products on the market labeled as personal care products that could kill you if you use them too much. Hard to believe but poisoning incidents with cosmetics/products for personal care represent approximately 9% of all inquiries to the Poisons Control Center in the United States. (This is closely followed by 8.6% for household cleaners.) I would venture to say that these incidents are probably severe allergic reactions (anaphylaxis) or ingestion (child ingests lipstick or such).

Personal products mostly include shampoos, makeup, deodorants, baby powders and hair spray. The list is literally endless. Each of these usually has a petroleum base, heavy metal (aluminum, mercury) or a noxious chemical (sodium lauryl sulfate). Remember what the oil spills in our oceans did to our fish and birds? That's what petroleum products do to our skin. They make the surface of our skin nice and soft but it prevents the cells from actually breathing. It is like wrapping your skin in plastic wrap. Not a pretty picture. Plus petroleum products will draw out the fat soluble vitamins from your skin which will ultimately make it age faster.

Our rule of thumb is: if it is toxic to ingest, then don't put it on your lips, skin or elsewhere. This is the same story that we already discussed with fluoride.

If you are looking for natural substitutes for personal care products, a little research on the internet will provide many. An excellent resource is http://www.earthclinic.com/.

- **Continuously detoxify and prevent further poison accumulation.**

The human brain forms and develops over a long period of time as compared to other organs, with rapid brain growth continuing throughout childhood. The blood brain barrier is not fully developed until much later in life, and even then, many toxins can still go through this barrier affecting the brain neurons. Heavy metals are definitely at the top of this list. In utero, the fetus has been found to get significant exposure to toxic substances through the maternal blood and across the placenta, with fetal metal toxicity levels often being higher than that of the mom. Also significant is that toxicity exposure has been found in children who were breastfed.

The incidence of neurotoxic or immune reactive conditions such as ADD, ADHD, autism, Aspergers, learning disabilities, asthma, allergies etc., has been increasing, sometimes exponentially, in recent years. Being labeled with these syndromes and given a medicine, does not guarantee a cure. It is up to us. Be proactive. Educate ourselves and take steps to secure our own health. Waiting for someone else to heal us is basically giving away our power. Remember you were born a lot healthier than you are presently. So, what happened between then and now?

1. Take soaking salt or clay baths once or twice a week. Baths are wonderfully healing, and it is easy to make your own homemade salt baths. Hot water relaxes the muscles and dilates the blood vessels, allowing more oxygen throughout the body. As more oxygen moves through the cells, you will automatically remove toxic wastes from the cells. The salt in the bath draws toxins out of the body to the skin's surface through a simple process of osmosis.

Using one half to one full cup of salt (Epsom, sea or Himalayan) will allow for detoxification. Other salts—all highly alkaline and cleansing—used in baths include baking soda and clay. All are good in different ways, so you should try to vary the salts in your baths. Notice how you feel after each, and do what makes you feel the best.

2. Try rebounding on a mini trampoline. When you use a rebounder, it promotes circulation through the body's lymphatic system. The toxins are moved to the lymph ducts, which transport the toxins to the kidney and liver, and ultimately out of the body. It is a great fun exercise and if done daily, will serve as an insurance policy against many serious diseases. It is a good way to get even the most sedentary Indigo moving. It is not only great exercise, but it is fun too. Sometimes I will do it with my favorite music or even while watching TV (if you must). The blood will flow, the toxins will go and the brain will glow! (Funny how I just came up with that).

3. Do oil pulling daily. Oil pulling is a simple Ayurvedic healing process for the oral cavity and the entire human body. It is great for acute infections of the mouth but therapeutic for chronic health challenges. One may have to practice oil pulling for months before long term results are noticed. It is valuable for purifying and strengthening the body. According to Ayurveda, organ meridians are present in the tongue just as they are in key points such of the hands, feet, ears and teeth.

Every organ in the human body is connected to other parts of the human body. We also know that each tooth and different parts of the tongue are associated with specific organs. As you heal the tooth and its environmental structures, the meridian associated organs will also heal. Its use will pull toxins from the mucus membranes of the mouth via the meridian system allowing for a complete body detoxification.

Traditionally, oil pulling has been used with sesame or sunflower oils, but has been modified recently to accommodate other oils and their healing properties. For general health purposes, I am partial to coconut oil due to its antibacterial, antifungal, antiviral properties. The oral cavity is full of bacteria, fungi and viruses. So it is great at keeping a healthy mouth and has been shown to remineralize tooth enamel. (Now we really have no reason to keep fluoride in our system.)

It is also a cooling oil and will work wonders on pulling out heat /congestion and assist in relieving infections, fevers, burns, cold sores, oral herpes outbreaks, and reduce overgrowth of Candida in the mouth. It may also alleviate the pain associated with these oral conditions. This is how you use it:

How to Oil Pull:

After thoroughly cleaning your teeth and gums, place approximately one tablespoon of organic virgin coconut oil in your mouth. The oil is put in the mouth, with chin tilted up, and slowly swished, sucked, chomped and pulled through the teeth for 15–20 minutes.

The oil changes from oily consistency to thin, white milky foam before spitting out. It is best to do it on an empty stomach, usually first thing in the morning before eating/drinking. (If the oil is still oily, it has not been pulled long enough.)

Then spit it out in the garbage or toilet. Do not spit the oil down the sink, as the oil will eventually clog your drain. Thoroughly rinse and wash your mouth with normal tap water.

Oil pulling should be done at least once a day, preferably in the morning on an empty stomach. No more than twice. Time constraints may be a factor, so it is a good thing to do in the shower, while reading, doing housework etc.

There are other benefits to coconut oil pulling:

- May stop tooth decay due to its antibacterial effects
- Will support periodontal health, may reverse gum infections
- Will help eradicate yeast infections in the mouth due to the presence of caprylic acid
- May whiten your teeth

- Facilitates absorption of calcium by the body; it helps in getting strong teeth and bones

Sunflower, sesame, olive and flax oils have been used with varying results. Best to try each of these oils for a short time period to see which works best for your specific condition.

4. Do dry body brushing. Dry skin brushing is one of the healthiest self-help methods available to us today. The best part is that it takes seconds to do, can be done in the comfort of your own home, and is painless and cost free.

Dry skin brushing promotes movement of the lymphatic system which can become stagnant or thick due to overload of toxins in the body or during an intense detoxification cleansing program. It will give your lymph system a kick start and help you feel refreshed and invigorated. Circulation improves, your skin becomes softer and healthier, and whole body wellness is enhanced. Your level of immunity increases and even common infections can be prevented.

How to Dry Skin Brush:

1. Purchase a natural, NOT a synthetic, bristle brush.

2. Purchase a brush with a long handle, so that you are able to reach all areas of your body.

3. Skin brushing should be performed once a day, preferably first thing in the morning. If you are feeling ill, please do it twice a day until you feel better.

4. Skin brushing should be performed prior to your bath or shower and your body should be dry. It might even be smart to do it while standing in the tub, so that dry skin can be washed away in the shower afterward.

5. Begin brushing your skin in long sweeping strokes starting from the bottom of your feet upwards, and from the hands towards the shoulders, and on the torso in an upward direction. Always brush towards the lymph glands so that toxins can be more easily released. Try and brush several times in each area, over-lapping as you go. *Note:* Major lymph glands are located under the jaw, at the underarms and in the groin areas. If this is too difficult to remember, then just brush towards the heart and 90% of the time you will be going in the right direction.

6. Avoid sensitive areas and anywhere the skin is broken. If anything hurts when you do it, then avoid those areas or do it gently until it becomes more tolerable.

7. For a thorough lymphatic cleansing, perform skin brushing daily for a minimum of three months.

Please do not skin brush if you have any varicose veins, painful rashes or open wounds.

Skin is the largest organ in the human body. It is responsible for one fourth of the body's detoxification, most of it through sweat. It eliminates two pounds of waste acids each day. So for those of us who are trying to be our healthiest, it would make sense to daily incorporate this simple detoxification technique.

Although not as popular, we have found that wet body brushing can be effective as well. It can be done in the shower or while soaking in a warm salt bath.

Everything that we have discussed in this chapter includes our basic do- it-yourself list for assisting you in handling the most common toxins. There is always more that can be done and I would advise everyone reading this to stay fully conscious and further explore the many other aspects to preventing and removing everyday poisons from your environment and your body.

Take back your power and do one new thing now; for the health of yourself and your children. By empowering yourself, and setting the example, you will inspire someone else.

We are all one. And by healing ourselves, we will heal others. I've seen this happen in my own life. And it can happen in yours.

Chapter Seven
* * *

Parents: Problems and Solutions

It is not because things are difficult that we do not dare; it is because we do not dare that things are difficult. – Seneca

Many of the problems that Indigos face may, in fact, be brought on by the parents. Caregivers, teachers and psychologists who mislabel children's psychic abilities or high sensitivities as vivid imagination or delusions, will only bring on emotional insecurity and intuitive shutting down. The Indigo will doubt her own credibility and possibly her own sanity. Acting out, learning disabilities, depression, or withdrawal are just a few of the symptoms that may result. Unfortunately, medication too often becomes the quick fix "cure".

Parents need to be their child's main support system. This is easier said than done. If you are a kid reading this and your parents could care less, so be it. You may actually be the older soul in the relationship and you need to educate your mom or dad. If this doesn't seem plausible, then it may be time to look outside for reputable holistic and metaphysical resources for support.

Sometimes, the lessons that we need to learn in this lifetime, may not be obvious. Learning to stand in your own power, discovering compassion for others, and knowing when to cut the ties to our ineffectual dismissive elders, is a tough life lesson. But occasionally we need to be the leader and set the example, even if we are the child. Maturity is not correlated with age. If you are reading this, you already know more than you give yourself credit for. When you tap into your inner brilliance and live an intuitive based life, others will be in awe of your accomplishments.

So I urge you, whether you are a parent or child, drop the labels, drop the gloom and doom. Rejoice in this miracle of who you are. Things will only get better from here. This chapter should give you some insights on parenting that can be utilized with all family members - parents and kids alike.

Parents and Anger Issues

Let's face it. If our parents don't support us, life only gets tough ... and at times, impossible. There have been many triumphant stories of kids who have had little support growing up or who got labeled with all kinds of learning disabilities and syndromes and yet still turned out quite successful. The story of Albert Einstein who never spoke before the age of 4, and accomplished so much, is classic.

Parents are not perfect. They don't always say the most supportive or nurturing comments to their children. As

Indigos, we tend to be more sensitive emotionally than just about everyone else. So if a comment is said our way that is not particularly positive, we are more likely to take it personally. The problem with this is that it ends up eating us up inside, and the final result is that we are more likely to react by making rash judgments about the insensitive person who made the comment. Or we might hold a grudge, or create an inaccurate belief system that becomes part of our very essence. And if these mental states of mind persist, it will create chronic problems with our health. And this is only because sometime in our past, someone said something hurtful, and it affected us on a very deep subconscious level. That means that you weren't even consciously aware of it. That is precisely why we are pointing it out to you.

We need to be conscious and alert, all the time if possible. Not an easy task considering that most of us are constantly being battered by subliminal messages from media (TV, magazines, newspapers, etc.), friends, family, teachers and religious leaders. Being a follower or a perfect child and wanting to fit in with the masses is expected and encouraged. Unfortunately, this will not fare well for the Indigo who is highly sensitive and intuitively wise.

An astute person once said that *being angry is like you taking arsenic and then waiting for the other person to die.* When we hold a grudge or continually stay angry, it messes up *our* energy fields. I am not just talking about the aura, but also the chakras (etheric energy fields within the body). This has a much deeper longer lasting effect on all our bodily organs in a detrimental way. The end result will be chronic health problems that will usually attract more low frequency energies that will bring us further into the abyss of chronic poor health. Didn't you ever notice that when you are angry you tend to be more accident prone, or that more bad news comes into your life? That is a vibrational match to your anger; so it would make great sense to consciously go out of your way and choose to be happy. Similar to when you choose what color outfit to wear; just choose a better state of mind.

Unfortunately, this low frequency energy of anger or depression will build on itself making us unbalanced, physically, mentally and emotionally. Ultimately, psychologically, this messes up our inherent belief systems. And yes, you too can grow up to become a miserable, cranky unhealthy adult.

So the time to create a strong base is now, before major damage is done and you have to undo a lifetime of resentment, anger and the cumulative effects of years of medication that you have been given to correct your labeled disabilities, mental state of depression and irrational behavior.

Everything Is Energy

We have all heard this concept before. Everything is energy. What this basically means is that we are all pretty much the same, and what really differentiates us from each other and from other living creatures is our energy or frequency.

There is a concept of epigenetics, where our environment can affect much of our genetic DNA expression. Dr. Bruce Lipton has elaborated on this in his book *The Biology of Belief: Unleashing the Power of Consciousness, Matter and Miracles*. I too, am a big believer that a healthy environment will produce a healthy child.

In physics there is an understanding that if two things have the same energy vibrations, they share "harmonic resonance," meaning that when one vibrates it causes the other to vibrate. For example, when a vocalist can sing the right note, one in tune with the atoms in a crystal goblet, their voice (vibration) can cause the goblet to shatter. The energy of the voice combines with the energy of the goblet's atoms and the two energies become so powerful together, it causes the goblet's atoms to fly apart and break the glass.

Some energies when added together become constructive, that is the two energies are summed together producing a more powerful vibratory energy. However, two energy waves can interact and cancel each other out, so when combined, the power of the combined energies becomes zero. In humans, when energies are constructive and give more power, we actually physically experience these energies as "good vibes." However, when two energies cancel each other out, we experience this energetically weakened state as "bad vibes."[1]

Building on a vibration of good nutrition, love and nurturance will usually culminate in an outcome more powerful than you have ever thought possible. I have seen this for myself firsthand. Our environment is so critical to regaining and maintaining excellent health.

This concept has also been explored by Dr. Masaru Emoto. He showed that when water was exposed to positive words like *love* and *happiness*, the water structure changed in a beneficial healthy way. Dr. Emoto froze positively exposed water and looked at the resulting crystals. He saw that this kind of water formed whole hexagonal water crystals. Actually, they were quite beautiful. He then showed that water that was exposed to negative words like *hate* and *war* formed warped crystals when frozen.

Dr. Emoto's conclusion was that words, intention or beliefs, spoken or otherwise, have an impact on you energetically. And when you realize that we are all at least seventy percent water, the results become even easier to understand. When someone else's words or actions create a negative emotion (anger, rage, depression, etc.) within you, there is a horrific effect on your body, mind and spirit.

Parents: Problems and Solutions

And since it is almost impossible to never be exposed to these low frequency environments, it is important to have techniques to release any low frequency energy that we may actually pick up. Protection for deflection is also important and this will be discussed in great detail in Chapter 8.

So for now, let's focus on the parent- child relationship and how we can enforce that to create a strong supportive environment.

On an energetic level, when there are negative belief systems, words or emotions, our auras and chakras lose their vibrant colors and become muddy brown looking.

Energetically, this is similar to when a car wheel gets stuck in deep mud and it is unable to move forward. Think- *stagnation of energy*. Depending upon where the brown is, in association with your body, it can cause congestion, physical pain or emotional discomfort. Obviously, it would be helpful to clear out that stuck energy.

On the chakra level, when exposed to the harmful frequency, the chakra can become closed down; either by not spinning or having no color or both. Being that the chakra is so assaulted, it is as if it is no longer there. Sounds weird but I have noticed this on many people. So, if we know which particular chakra has the issue, we can help reverse the process.

On an etheric level, when we are in a low emotional state (being angry, mad, upset) we attract more low frequency entities/energies. The low frequency energies take power from us; it is like they are feeding off of us. As a result, we could physically feel drained or lethargic. We may notice a tendency toward bad luck and we are more likely to get sick with a cold, get in accidents or hurt ourselves by mistake. On an emotional level we could feel more depressed than ever.

These energies that we have picked up could be lost souls of deceased people or possible alien low frequency energies. Once they are removed, we bring our own energy level to a higher vibration. Sometimes the energies will leave if we just ground ourselves, detox and keep ourselves in an upbeat positive health promoting environment. If they no longer resonate with our vibration, they will move on until they find a new accommodating individual.

Our belief systems are something we choose. At first it might seem that we have no control since these are ingrained within us since birth; but in reality, we do. This is when affirmations come in handy, along with EFT (Emotional Freedom Technique) and NLP (NeuroLinguistic Programming). These are tools discussed in Chapter 8 that will help us release old beliefs and assume new ones that are more supportive and vibrationally uplifting.

Open Parent - Child Communication

Parents need to be their child's support. One way to do this is through proper word choice, especially with regard to intuitive abilities.

When you are emphasizing intuition in your child, you are really supporting their true self. The true self could be defined as who they are, not what society or others expect them to be. Falling into the trap of believing your child is not good enough, not smart enough or not pretty enough, just because some "expert with credentials" said so, is selling out on your child. As we have said before, your child is perfect, and don't let anyone else tell you otherwise. It is your responsibility to nurture the best from your child, and then sit back in awe at the wonderment of how you were blessed with this beautiful being.

Let me start by saying that neither my mom nor I have any degrees in psychology. But we do have a great deal of experience in dealing with all personalities of people. We have taken a myriad of classes on emotional and energetic self healing and have come a long way in resolving some family and life issues for ourselves and others as well. These basic techniques have worked extraordinarily well and we are so happy to share them with you. What we have found is that not always one technique will resolve the problem. But by implementing as many as you can, shifting can occur. Sometimes even miracles.

So what do you do when your family member gets on your nerves? Before you answer this with a negative response and bring that kind of energy into your field, try this suggestion first:

It is always paramount that you get yourself out of the room or space where the conflict person is. It is also best not to respond to the parent/child if what they are saying is negative.

Basically the rule is:

IF YOU CAN'T SAY ANYTHING NICE, DO NOT SAY ANYTHING AT ALL!

If you have an irresistible urge to respond, then simply say: "Thank you for sharing." Smile and walk away.

This sentence, "Thank you for sharing," is used to defuse the situation. You are acknowledging the person but are basically saying something neutral to what they say. It's active listening at its best. Acknowledge them, but don't get involved.

If you are still angry, upset, sad, or depressed, there are a few tricks that you can apply until things are calmer and to help transmute this negative emotion to a higher frequency.

Trick #1: The Journal

Keep a journal. Journal writing means that you write down your thoughts and experiences on a regular basis. This will help you keep track of your own emotional growth as a person. It will also help you to release some pent up emotions and to clarify your personal goals.

Trick #2: The Letter

This is your opportunity to really get everything off your chest. Write exactly how you are feeling in a letter to the person that upset you. Include everything, details, events and even profanity if needed. It all has to come out.

This is helpful to get these emotions out of your head and onto the paper. Pinpoint who you are angry at. Explain why you're angry, how you feel about this person and any other things you wish to say to their face but can't.

The rule I put in before -" *IF YOU CAN'T SAY ANYTHING NICE, DO NOT SAY ANYTHING AT ALL!"* does not apply here.

Once you are done writing all you need to write, you need to end the letter with the words "I forgive you."

Forgiveness is a difficult emotion to express when someone has hurt you. But it is needed so that you can move on. If you do not forgive that person, they will always have power over you and be able to manipulate you emotionally.

Finally, you must destroy the letter. Yes, you read right – destroy the letter. It will not do you or the other person any good if they actually read it. If anything, it will probably incite them again and escalate the bad emotions to an even higher level. The best way to destroy the letter is to burn it, rip it into a million pieces, bury it or throw it in the garbage. Personally, I've done a combination of all of these.

If you find that any emotion continues to come up again, then you can write them another letter elaborating on the further details of your angst. Again, you must destroy the letter.

Trick #3: Send Love
The frequency of love is very powerful. Even though you might be feeling hate for this person, feeling more hate does not improve the circumstance. As many of us already know, hate is really not the emotion in question here. It is really the absence of love.

You need to elevate the situation to a higher frequency by putting them in white light and then send them love. This may be an emotionally tough thing to do if you haven't done Trick #1 and #2 first.

To send them love can be perceived as surrounding them in hearts or angels or having a cute puppy licking them. You can even see them as a baby being cuddled by their mommy. Basically imagine anything that resonates for you. It is the intention that makes this trick work, not the actual imagery.

Parents: Problems and Solutions

You must feel it in your heart as real as you can possibly make it. If you find it tough to send them this love energy, it will be helpful if you ground yourself and send love to your own self first. Then when you are feeling more at ease, try sending love to them. It should work.

Do this exercise for at least ten minutes or longer. You will notice the shift. Not only in you, but in the other person as well.

Trick #4: Feel Gratitude
Just like love, *gratitude* is a high frequency. Having gratitude for the positive memories, lessons learned, and experiences you have, is one step closer to forgiveness.

Say or think the sentence: *I am grateful for*_____.

Just fill in the blank. Do this exercise as often as you can for as long as you can; for at least ten minutes or longer. It almost becomes a form of meditation and can create an inner peace like no medication could ever possibly achieve.

I often use this as a walking meditation. *"What beautiful trees. Thank you for being here and cleaning our air and making the street lovelier. ... What a beautiful building. So tall and majestic. Wow. And look at the pretty architecture. ... The clouds. They're so puffy and white. Thank you for providing rain for the plants to grow and giving us water to drink..... And look at that beautiful big pile of garbage on the street. Somebody just cleaned out their home to make room for new stuff……And those dirty pots and dishes left in the sink. So grateful to have such healthy food to eat on these lovely dishes."*

You get the point. Find the joy of everything. It's there if you change your paradigm viewpoint.

While the old adage says to count sheep if you can't sleep, I say to count blessings. Not only will you fall asleep quicker, you will be in a very restful high frequency state of tranquility. Your dreams will be better and you will wake up more refreshed than ever. The added bonus is that you will see your life attracting more positive experiences. It's a paradigm shift of focusing on what you have and not on what you want. The *Universal Law of Attraction* will always bring more of whatever you think about.

If you worry incessantly on how your parents are mean, guess what? They will be. But if you show gratitude for all the nice things they have done (given you food, clothing, toys, life, etc.) then you will find that they will continue to do more of it.

And for the parents, if you worry and continue to point out how inadequate your child is relative to other kids his age, then you will never see the blessings of their situation. Not everyone can be a doctor, lawyer or rocket scientist, so focus on their strengths and show gratitude for your child's gifts.

Parents: Problems and Solutions

Trick #5: Be Grounded
When you are grounded, you are able to think clearer and are able to forgive.

Hold on to a house plant, rock or crystal. Walk barefoot on the grass or beach. Hug a tree. When you connect to the Earth and resonate with her energy, you will find yourself in a natural flow of life and less likely to lose your temper. You will also be able to think clearer.

There is a lot to be said about grounding, and by far this may be the single most important thing to do to reclaim your mind, health and power.

Great detail on grounding will be in Chapter 8.

Trick #6: Walk
Walking is a great exercise. Besides giving you a change of scenery, it will also help you let off some steam through the production of endorphins (the happy hormone). The more you walk, the better you will feel mentally and emotionally.

When you take a walk, the new environment will give you a new perspective on any situation. Walk to a place that will give you peace; there's the park, pet store or library.

Parks are a great place that you can connect with nature and ground yourself. As you gaze at the trees, grass, flowers and wildlife, your mood can't help but shift. If you rub your bare feet and hands into the grass, you will find that your tension is releasing. Sit there for at least twenty minutes.

If you have a pet, take it for a walk, read to it, and play with it. I have lost count on the number of times that my parents got me extremely mad, but the instant I hold my dog and look into those eyes, I feel so much better. Animals are so naturally grounded since they always walk barefoot on the earth. So if you can hold a pet, you will find your energy shifting.

Even window shopping can be transformative. Just don't buy anything as this may create regret or upset later.

Trick #7: Use Your Imagination
Read a book. If written well, they can quickly help lift you out of your distressed mood. Libraries are filled with resources. The wonderful part about books is that they take you on a journey. They allow you to live other people's lives and teach you how to navigate in our world.

Get involved in creative projects. Music, art, dance and sports are a wonderful release and distraction from day to day annoyances. Just do not use it as an escape from your family situation. It is there to keep you in balance.

By the way, watching television is NOT using your imagination.

Parents: Problems and Solutions

Trick #8: Breathe

Deep breathing is so often overlooked. The deeper you breathe the more oxygen will go throughout your body. This will give you a chance to relax, as it releases tension and elevates your mood. Your mind will clear and allow you to rethink what should be the next step.

Try to inhale into the base of your abdomen. This way you know that you will be using maximum lung capacity and will receive maximum oxygen supply throughout your body. And when your cells get more oxygen, you will become calmer. Not to mention you will even improve your physical and mental health.

Trick #9: Eat Healthy

Indigos are more sensitive than most people. Read labels. If you can't pronounce any of the ingredients listed, then it is probably a toxic chemical. It will affect not only your physical health but your emotional health as well. My mom always says that if the food comes in a box with a list of ingredients that you can't pronounce, chances are that it's not good for you. Most likely it is not real food but processed chemicals creating pseudo-food. It's very deceptive since it may smell and look like the real deal but it is completely artificial. Yuck!

Be smart. Eat organic and as natural as possible.
As for the parents, you need to set the example. Chances are that you are not as sensitive as your child, and you probably

will continue to eat your junk food. Just don't let your kid see it. Better yet, you too can eat smarter and you both can experience phenomenal health and vitality together.

Final Thoughts

We are all human. We are all one. Treat you family member as you would like to be treated. If you feel the overwhelm of emotion rising up, or the hopelessness of the situation, you need to take a step back and do whatever you can to help the other person as you would want to be helped. These few simple tricks in this chapter may be the quick fix answer. If not, then deeper solutions are coming up next in Chapter 8.

Problem people do not have to be problems. They present challenges for us so that we can tap into our own wisdom to do the right thing. My mom has often said, "Will you do the right thing or the easy thing?" I try to live by these words as the "right thing" is usually the better long term solution even though it may be the more difficult thing. The "easy thing" is just a temporary bandage, and sooner or later the whole problem just blows up again into something bigger and more troublesome.

Stop the blame game. Pointing fingers at someone else as the cause of your unhappiness is not a solution. If you are feeling distraught, it is *your* choice for *you* to release this upset energy. No one can say, or do anything to change *your* mind.

It is called *free will*. Only *you* have complete control of *your* emotions.

The same goes when someone is mad at you. They have a right to feel how they feel. I did not say it was a just cause to hold this anger as they do, but they too have free will. When you give the person space, let them know that you are there for them if they would like to talk, and send them love (Trick #3), that will be enough to let the person know that they have support. Eventually, most times, they come around. It may not be as soon as you had hoped, but there is a Divine plan.

Believe that everything is working out exactly as it is supposed to. And no amount of yelling or screaming will expedite it. When you do the "right thing", there is no more you can do.

---

[1] *"Interview with Bruce in Planeta Magazine - Part 2." Uncovering the Biology of Belief.* Bruce Lipton, 09/15/08. Web. <http://www.brucelipton.com/interviews/interview-with-bruce-in-planeta-magazine-part-2/>.

Chapter Eight
* * *
Own Your Power

Success is not final, failure is not fatal: it is the courage to continue that counts. -Winston Churchill

It is often said that it takes a village to raise a child. And this statement holds even more truth when you have an Indigo Child. A supportive family is a good foundation but neighbors and teachers are an important part of the equation. There will always be many challenges in life, and let's face it, we need all the help we can get.

If we want this kind of support, the place to begin is with ourselves. Community, like charity, begins at home. You start building a good neighborhood when you yourself decide that you will be a good neighbor. If you don't know anyone in your building or on your block, you can take the initiative. The classic Hopi expression "You be the leader that you are looking for," applies here perfectly. If you are waiting for someone else to reach out to you, you may be waiting a very long time.

There are endless stories of neighbors living right next door to each other for decades and never saying hello until something bad happens. Don't wait. Set the example and know that you have a support system in place if you should need it. Better yet, you have a friend within a few steps of your own home. You can bake some cookies and take them to your neighbors and introduce yourself. You can join a church or temple and become part of that community. You can reach out to create your own network of friends and start building community.

It's nice to have friends and neighbors to rely on. But what do you do if your friends, neighbors and family are more irksome than uplifting? Life can get pretty lonely if you start to disown everybody. Plus, it will start to look a little suspicious if you keep turning down invitations to family and social gatherings. These people may mean well, but if you leave these encounters feeling mentally down and physically ill, then you seriously need to work on your personal boundaries. Owning your own power is a learning process that we all go through sometime in our lives, but for super sensitive Indigos, it's a major deal that can make a significant difference in quality of life.

Here are the basics that will work wonders.

- **Ground Yourself Daily**

Electropollution or electromagnetic smog is a new phenomenon that needs some serious discussion. Non-ionizing electromagnetic radiation propagated through the atmosphere by broadcast towers, satellite dishes, radar installations, microwave appliances, cell phones, computers and the magnetic fields surrounding electrical appliances and power lines, are believed to have injurious effects on people and the environment. Electrical overload can have a cumulative serious harmful effect on the human body, creating all kinds of dis-ease.

Earthing

In the book *Earthing*, renowned cardiologist, Stephen Sinatra, M.D. says, "I regard Earthing as the greatest health breakthrough in all my years in medical practice. Regular grounding (another name for Earthing) restores the body's natural electrical state, calms the nervous system, reduces inflammation, and improves circulation. No pill on Earth can do what Mother Earth does!"[1]

Personally, we have found that grounding ourselves daily is probably the easiest and most important health promoting action that can be done to give the most positive outcome. And if you are wondering why, here are the reasons.

Earth's background base frequency, or "heartbeat," (Schumann Resonance) is rising dramatically. It may vary among geographical regions but the overall measurement was 7.8 cycles per second (hertz) for many decades. This measurement was once thought to be a constant; global military communications developed on this frequency. However, recent reports set the rate at over 11 hertz, and still climbing. Science does not have a clear answer as to why this is happening, or even what to make of it.

There has been data collected by the Norwegian and Russian researchers on this but it's not widely reported in the U.S. The only reference to Schumann Resonance is found in the Seattle Library reference section and it is tied to the weather. Science acknowledges Schumann Resonance as a sensitive indicator of temperature variations and worldwide weather conditions. It is believed that the escalating Schumann Resonance may be a factor in the many recent intense Earth shifts. The frequency of earthquakes, tsunamis, storms, floods, and extreme weather is definitely on the rise.

So how does this affect us? If a planet's frequency is rising, then the frequency of the inhabitants of that planet must also rise. We cannot live comfortably or healthily on a planet that we do not resonate with. Knowing this, it is important to reconnect to the Earth as much as possible. If not, you will be ill, physically, mentally and emotionally ill. Living in boxes (houses, apartment buildings), driving in boxes (cars) and working in boxes (office buildings) have literally kept us disconnected from earth. Even when we do go out in nature, most of the time we are wearing rubber soled shoes that further insulate us from earth.

Earthing allows a transfer of electrons (the Earth's natural, subtle energy) into the body. We know that inflammation is caused by free radicals and that free radicals are neutralized with electrons from any source. Electrons are the source of the neutralizing power of antioxidants.[1]

There are several things that happen when you ground yourself.

1. Reduction of pain.
2. Reduction of anxiety.
3. Emotional detoxification.
4. Reduction of cortisol levels and resynchronizing its secretion to be in alignment with the natural 24-hour circadian rhythm profile. This will create less stress and better sleep for deeper healing.
5. Increased fluidity of red blood cells allowing more oxygen transport to all parts of the body.

Grounding is very simple to do and if done for 20 minutes or longer daily, you will see your whole life shift for the better.

It can be achieved by simply wiggling your toes and deep breathing. But it is best accomplished by connecting directly to Mother Earth. It is good to run barefoot in the grass, soil or sand. "Hug a tree" comes to mind as well. Perhaps even jumping into the ocean (literally) and letting the salt water wash away all the stresses of the day. If this is not possible, try salt baths at home. Sea salt, Himalayan salt or Epsom salt is usually best for this. Clay or mud baths are another possibility. Holding onto large houseplants or grounding stones (obsidian, rose quartz, etc.) for 10 to 15 minutes a day will also help you to feel more centered.

My mom and I were taking an energy healing course. The teacher was pompous and had an arrogant personality. She made it seem that no one was quite as good an intuitive as she was. She claimed she was working with Energies of Light. Then when she found out that I was able to talk directly to the angelic realm and beyond, she became attached and somewhat obsessed with me. She, instead of one of my fellow classmates, performed the energy attunement activation on me.

After the course, when we were going home, my mom asked me a question to ask the angels. I attempted to contact them but there was nothing. Now that was unusual. I had already known about Azul (my etheric twin), so I asked him what was going on. Azul said that the class instructor had attempted to cut me off and block me from the angels. It was not that she had so much divine power to do so; it was that she had teamed up with low frequencies to help her out.

Some of you might be wondering why the angels would allow this to happen. From a separate and similar experience (see Chapter 5), I have learned (again and again) that sometimes the angels will let experiences like this happen, to help us learn a lesson.

On this occasion, Azul, being the smart etheric twin that he is, said that if I connected with nature and grounded myself, this blockage would clear. So my mom and I found a park lawn with a beautiful solid tree and connected to the earth for about two hours. After about an hour, I was able to communicate with the angelic realm again. It was a bit fuzzy (both visual and auditory) but by about an hour and a half into this grounding with tapping and deep breathing, things were returning to normal.

I developed a new respect for Azul and I also learned that not all intuitive energy teachers are good, even if they claim to be so. And most importantly, I learned that if I return to my grounding, I will always find my way. Mother Earth is very nurturing and very wise. –Diandra

Music

Another way to ground is through sound. Henry Wadsworth Longfellow has said that "Music is the universal language of mankind," and I whole heartedly agree. Playing classical music or CDs of the ocean, nature, humpback whales, birds or the like, may induce a deeply tranquil state allowing your child to function better, think clearer and sleep more soundly. I have also found that many of these high frequency (especially the whales) sounds, will also energetically clear space.

There are also audio guidance CDs (Hemi Sync®) that safely alter brainwave patterns by using multi-layered guides of sound frequencies. When you hear these through stereo headphones or speakers, the brain responds by producing a third sound (called a binaural beat) that encourages the desired brainwave activity. This will help you tap into more of your brain's innate abilities, reduce stress, increase concentration and experience deep, restorative sleep. It may even help you uncover intuitive talents.

Breathe

Many years ago, I heard a story that really stuck with me. It seems that upon autopsy, it was found that most people have atrophied lower half of their lungs. Theory has it that this occurs due to the superficial breathing that we are all doing. This is such a shame to have your lungs wither away due to lack of use.

The lesson learned from this story is that we all need to be consciously aware of how we are breathing and intentionally do deep breathing exercises on a daily basis.

The benefits of diaphragmatic breathing are many. Here's the short list.

1. Breathing increases the amount of oxygen in your body.

Oxygen attaches to hemoglobin in your red blood cells. This in turn enriches your body to metabolize nutrients and vitamins. By doing this, it will improve cellular regeneration, relieve pain and strengthen the immune system.

2. Breathing releases tension.
   This in turn will relax the mind/body and reduce anxiety.

3. Breathing massages your organs: the stomach, small intestine, liver and pancreas. Digestion and detoxification will improve. The upper movement of the diaphragm also massages the heart, leading to an increase in circulation, thus allowing less stress on the heart.

   When you inhale, your diaphragm descends and your abdomen will expand. By this action you massage vital organs and improve circulation. Controlled breathing also strengthens and tones your abdominal muscles.

4. Breathing releases toxins.
   Your body is designed to release 70% of its toxins through breathing. If you are not breathing effectively, you are not properly ridding your body of its toxins. This means that other systems in your body must work overtime which could eventually lead to

illness. When you exhale air from your body you release carbon dioxide that has been passed through from your bloodstream into your lungs. Carbon dioxide is a natural waste of your body's metabolism.

5. Breathing moves stuck energy.
   Most people are walking around practically holding their breath. We have all experienced the after effects of exhaling a big breath. It may feel like someone just took a hundred pound weight off our shoulders. It relieves muscle tension, emotional problems and clears uneasy feelings out of the body. For these reasons, deep breathing is always used during any of our energy healing sessions. If you ground yourself at the same time, the effects are exponential.

6. Breathing improves the nervous system, the brain and the spinal cord.
   Nerves receive increased oxygenation and are more nourished. This improves the health of the whole body, since the nervous system communicates to all parts of the body.

7. Breathing improves posture.
   Good breathing techniques over a sustained period of time will encourage good posture. The chest expands, the shoulders go up and the abdomen tightens. The entire body works more efficiently, assisting in attaining ideal weight.

- **Emotional Release**

Neuro-Lingistic Programming (NLP) and Emotional Freedom Technique (EFT) are two amazing modalities for releasing emotional issues that are causing physical or mental problems. We've used them both, sometimes consecutively within the same session to achieve release of problematic issues that may be resistant to releasing.

NLP

NLP stands for Neuro-Linguistic Programming, a name that encompasses the three most influential components involved in producing human experience: *neurology, language* and *programming*. The neurological system regulates how our bodies function, language determines how we interface and communicate with other people and our programming determines the kinds of models of the world we create. It describes the fundamental dynamics between mind (neuro) and language (linguistic) and how their interplay affects our body and behavior (programming).

NLP was originated by John Grinder (whose background was in linguistics) and Richard Bandler (whose background was in mathematics and Gestalt therapy) for the purpose of making explicit models of human excellence. Grinder and Bandler formalized their modeling techniques and their own individual contributions under the name *"Neuro-Linguistic Programming"* to symbolize the relationship between the brain, language and the body. The basics of this model has been described in a series of books including *Frogs Into Princes* (Bandler & Grinder, 1979), *Neuro Linguistic Programming Vol. 1* (Dilts, Grinder, Bandler, DeLozier, 1980), *Reframing,* (Bandler & Grinder, 1982) and *Using Your Brain* (Bandler, 1985). Although these books are excellent resources to learn more, we suggest seeing a certified practitioner to get real results.

Through the years, NLP has developed some very fast, effective and powerful tools for creating change in a wide range of professional and personal areas including: health, counseling, psychotherapy, education, creativity, leadership and parenting.

It allows you to reframe anything in your life: relationships, health, school, work, finances. By reframing the event in your mind, the emotional impact literally disappears. When you remember or retell your "story", grief, fear or anger will no longer be part of it. Now it will just come up as an event that happened. The emotional charge attached to it is gone.

There are immense intricacies to how it can be done, so it is important to either pursue further education in its use or find a qualified practitioner who can help you in shifting the disquieting emotional events in your life.

But here is a simple example of how we used it.

Remember the story that Diandra retold in Chapter 2 about her kindergarten teacher? It had a tremendous effect on her personal self esteem and safety at the time. Years later, she would still feel physically and emotionally ill when recalling the kindergarten teacher. So this is how we approached it. After you have your child in a comfortable relaxed position, try this.

Take a deep breath. Feel the cushion of the chair under you and know that you are safe and secure. See Ms. X (kindergarten teacher). She is screaming and turning all different shades of red. It almost looks like she has a tomato face. Let us see her differently. Imagine her head changing into Mickey Mouse. Now look at her Mickey Mouse ears. Yes. Big and cartoonish. Let's put a red jacket with 2 big blue buttons on her. Do you see her Mickey Mouse tail wiggling behind her? And look at that big round black nose. She's actually getting funnier looking by the minute. Oh, and her voice. The more she screams, the squeakier it gets, just like Mickey Mouse.

Now see her head with her big humongous Mickey Mouse ears? Her entire head is getting smaller and smaller. Her head is so tiny, her mouth is so tiny, her voice is so tiny.....just a little squeaky mouse going on and on with her little squeaky voice. You can hardly hear her. Her entire body is getting smaller and smaller.

Let's put her on a puffy white cloud. How happy she looks on her puffy white cloud, just squeaking and squeaking away. And here comes Mr. Wind just blowing along. And with one big "Poof!" the cloud with Mickey Mouse -Ms. X is all gone!

I can guarantee you that if you try this with your child, the entire traumatic event will never be the same to them. There may still be some residual unfinished pieces to work through, but the bulk of the emotional charge will be gone.

Typically, we all have had emotionally charged experiences with horrific teachers, employers, relatives and even strangers. We usually manage it by just letting the memory "go." The question is "go" where? Somewhere in everyone is a repressed bad emotional memory that we think we have forgotten about or dismissed as something unimportant, because it was so long ago and not really significant to recall it. But you know, sometime in your life, that memory will come to the surface and haunt you. Usually it manifests with seeing a therapist for years to work out your problems. Or with minor self talk of "I'm not good enough, smart enough or pretty enough." Or someone says or does something that pushes your buttons and you become an emotional mess or burst out in anger.

NLP will help relieve this. My next choice is EFT.

EFT

Emotional Freedom Technique (EFT) was originally created to be used in the psychotherapy profession. Presently, its use is universal. It is based on a revolutionary discovery that violates most of the beliefs held within conventional psychology. It contends that the cause of all negative emotions is a disruption in the body's energy system (chi, ki or prana). It is a form of acupressure that uses gentle tapping to stimulate traditional Chinese acupuncture points. This mapping out of our energy acupuncture points dates back 5,000 years.

Tapping on specific points of the face and body is combined with identifying the problem, followed by a general phrase of affirmation. With EFT, the body's subtle energy systems become balanced and there appears to be relief from emotional stress and physical discomfort.

With remarkable consistency, EFT relieves symptoms by an unusual routine of tapping with the fingertips on a short series of points on the body that correspond to acupuncture points on the energy meridians. Where there is an imbalance, there is a corresponding blockage in the flow of energy through the meridian system.

This technique has helped our clients as well as us.

I will briefly describe a basic recipe for using the tapping technique. There are many variations of this recipe and you can further modify it to suit your situation.

Please keep in mind that EFT is not meant to replace standard medical or psychological care/counseling. Although this technique may not have documentation of negative side effects, this does not mean you may not experience any side effects at all. Usually some emotional release (crying or deeper sadness or even anger) will occur with EFT, so you must be prepared to deal with that as well. If these emotions do occur, then you are probably tapping on the right points with the right affirmations. It can become intense and perhaps overwhelming. That is why we recommend working with a certified practitioner of EFT. The results can be life changing in miraculous ways.

The following is a list of points that can be tapped on.

- On the top of the head, the crown.
- At the beginning of the eyebrow, just above and to one side of the nose.
- On the bone bordering the outside corner of the eye.
- On the bone under an eye about one inch below your pupil.
- On the small area between the bottom of your nose and the top of your upper lip.
- On the chin area below your lower lip.

- The chest under the clavicle.
- The underarm.
- The last point is the karate chop point. It is located in the middle of the fleshy part on the outside of the hand between the top of the wrist bone and the base of the baby finger.
- There are additional points on the fingers but for the sake of simplicity, we will leave those out. Further information on the use of all points can be attained through the many books written on EFT, classes, and of course, the internet. Much can be learned through watching YouTube videos on the subject.

Basic recipe:

1. Setup statement: Name the problem combined with an affirmation phrase.

   The traditional EFT phrase uses the following setup:

   "Even though I have this _____,
   I deeply and completely accept myself."

   The blank in the first sentence above is filled in with a brief description of the negative emotion or problem that you want to address.

   You can also substitute other positive conclusions as the second part of the phrase:

> *"I deeply and completely love and accept myself."*
> *"I deeply and profoundly accept myself."*
> *"I'm a really wonderful person and I deserve better."*
> *"I'm an amazing kid and I deserve better."*

Others may work as well, but these are fairly universal.

2. Start on the karate chop point and tap at least ten times while restating the setup statement. You can state the problem and an affirmation out loud (three times).

3. Sequence: Most EFT courses will teach you to use all energy points of the face and body and tap at least ten times in a specific sequence.

4. Repetition: Positive tapping sequence continues with each facial energy point. The focus is now on the positive results that you will be experiencing and new outcomes.

You will find that some points will elicit an emotional response and others will appear to do nothing. As you are doing this tapping with the affirmation, emotions may come up. Best thing to do is keep working through it and continue to deep breathe simultaneously to keep the energy moving.

Also, you may notice that a new aspect of the problem may arise. You should continue to tap with the new aspects being morphed into the affirmation phrase.

For example, with Diandra's kindergarten teacher Ms. X:

Starting at the Karate point and working our way from the crown through the face, chest, karate point, crown through the face, chest, karate point, etc.

Even though Ms. X is a mean teacher, I completely love and accept myself.

Say this at each point once with at least 10 taps at each point. Then do the same for each additional affirmation:

Even though Ms. X screams loud at the kids in the class, I completely love and accept myself.

Even though Ms. X is scary looking when she screams, I completely love and accept myself.

Even though Ms. X is a teacher and teachers are supposed to be nice, and she isn't, I completely love and accept myself.

Even though I was in Ms. X's class, that doesn't mean that I deserved to have her, since I completely love and accept myself.

As you can see, the list of affirmations can go on and on, especially as new aspects of the same problem rise to the surface, as you work through the layers.

Points to keep in mind:

- It is best to say it out loud, but if you are in a social situation where you prefer to mutter it under your breath or do it silently...then go ahead. It will still be effective.
- It is better to say it with feeling and emphasis, but just saying it will usually do the job.
- It doesn't matter whether you believe the affirmation or not. By just saying it, you will stir up the meridian system and get something moving.

Hard to believe, but we have even done this on ourselves to shift other people and it still works!

It's always time for a miracle. The tapping technique can create this.

- **Vision Boards**

Everyone has a dream, Indigos included. And for many of us, it may be difficult to put it into written or spoken words. We can see it in our head but it doesn't manifest into real 3D life. Now it can with a Vision Board.

Manifestation Boards or Vision Boards are effective at getting you focused and clear at getting you what you want. They are fun to make and usually bring up personal happiness when you continue to look at them.
It can be very elaborate with colorful decorations or quite simple on a sheet of plain paper. You can even create one on the computer (make it a screen saver) if that is what works best for you. The main thing is to post it in a place where you can see it every day, so that you can look at it and feel its energy.

Basically you are creating a collage of pictures, words and thoughts of what you would like to accomplish or attain: like an A+ on you next exam, a new desk or house or job, or pictures and attributes of people you would like to have as your friends. You can even place a check made out to yourself for a million dollars.

Here's a simple example of a Vision Board for those who want to lose some weight. Take a photo of your head and put it on the photo of the body you want. You can place this picture on the refrigerator or in your clothes closet. It will be a quick reminder of what you can look like when you are at your ideal weight. If you keep it realistic, it should work.

You can have a board for school, another for work, and even a third one for personal desires. Or make a really big board with everything on it.

And now that it is sitting there in a place where you can see it every day, you can't help but use it.

See all these accomplishments in your mind's eye, hold it, feel it, and let it resonate through you until you feel it in your core. Feel the happy energy rise within you, knowing that you are creating a wonderful life for yourself and that these desires are coming true. Feel the gratitude of all that you have already accomplished, and thank the Universe (or whomever you believe in) for giving you these wonderful things. When you feel it as if it's already there, it will be. That's the Law of Attraction doing its job; believing is seeing.

Thoughts might come into your head as you focus on your board. That's perfect. Write down on paper or in a notebook planner these thoughts on what you need to do to create this life that you want to live. A plan of action *in writing* will make a world of difference. Do something to make it happen, and it will.

If you spend at least 10 minutes once a day, your life should shift in a short period of time. Doing it early in the day is usually best. If done too late in the day, it may be forgotten or it may keep you up at night, since your mind will be racing and planning how to put your thoughts into action.

This should be a fun project; as the energy you put into it, will be exactly what you get out of it. If it feels like a chore, then don't do it. You might want to work on some of the other techniques that we mention in this book. Once you are more grounded and energetically clearer, the Vision Board will come easily. Moving forward can sometimes be scary, so excuses can be many. If we thought this Vision Board exercise was stupid or a waste of time, this book you're reading would not exist. This *Enlightened Indigo Child* book that you are reading was on Diandra's Vision board and then mine.

The Law of Attraction rules. If you can believe something/anything in your core, the Universe will deliver. The Vision Board is there to keep you on track to accomplishing your goals.

Most Indigos are procrastinators, so we are here to remind you that **you** need to be proactive for you, if anything is to change. The unseen universal forces of love and light (the quantum field) will support you. Always.

▪ Learning Styles

Even though we didn't put a lot of attention to this topic as a support for Diandra's schoolwork, we feel that it is worth bringing attention to.

There are three main types of learning styles: auditory, visual, and kinesthetic. Most people learn best through a combination of the three types of learning styles and they usually have a clear preference for one.

It is advantageous to understand your type of learning style so that homework and learning may become easier and less stressful. If you know what learning style you are, you can work with a special trained therapist teacher who can help you master skills specifically geared for your learning style. Learning should and could be a joy. Attitude is very important for success at school or life in general.

There are no poor students, just poor teachers. We need to look out for our child's best interest. In a classroom with many students, the teachers may not have the time or patience or knowledge to help your special Indigo Child. Actually, the teacher probably doesn't even know what an Indigo Child is (might want to lend her this book). To her, your child is disruptive, slow or not right. And she will be the first one to say your child probably needs a prescription drug to make it better. I think not!

I believe it's time to look outside the conventional box.

Auditory Learners: Hear
Auditory learners would rather listen to things being explained than read about them. Reciting information out loud and having music in the background may be a common study method. Other noises may become a distraction resulting in a need for a relatively quiet place. Auditory

learners will benefit from creating recordings of the information that is being taught, as well as benefit from information that has been played back from these recordings. Most auditory learners tend to repeat things aloud, so they are able to easily learn the information that is being repeated.

Visual Learners: See
Visual learners learn best by looking at graphics, watching a demonstration, or reading. For them, it's easy to look at charts and graphs, but they may have difficulty focusing while listening to an explanation. If you take notes when visual information is being presented, and create your own charts and graphics while learning, then you may be a visual learner. Through the use of hand-outs, charts and visual information, the visual learner should be easily able to readily absorb the information.

Kinesthetic Learners: Touch
Kinesthetic learners process information best through a hands-on experience. Clairvoyant Indigos do best with this style. It keeps them present in the here and now. Actually doing an activity can be the easiest way for them to learn. Sitting still while studying may be difficult, but writing things down makes it easier to understand. There are many approaches that tactile learners can take while trying to master new skills. Tactile learners can use a hands-on approach to take part in experiments, as well as other experiential approaches where the individual can be involved in the learning.

A well-balanced child is able to develop all three types of learning styles. Just because a child has a dominant learning style doesn't mean that the other types can't be improved. Having just one dominant learning style, and relying on that style only, can debilitate a child's true potential. There are many different ways to train in the different types of learning styles, but it ultimately comes down to training the cognitive skills. Cognitive skills are the foundational building blocks of each learning style. Without properly trained cognitive skills, a child isn't able to use or take advantage of the other learning styles effectively.

There are many specialty centers that can evaluate your child to see what works best for them. It is definitely worth doing if your Indigo has challenges in school. The real work begins with developing skills and strategies that work with your child's style for her educational success. It can be done.

Keep the faith.

---

[1] Earthing Institute, Inc., "Earthing Research." *Earthing Institute*. 2012. Web.
<http://www.earthinginstitute.net/index.php/research >.

Chapter Nine
* * *
Where Do We Go From Here?

Children are the world's most valuable resource and its best hope for the future. - John Fitzgerald Kennedy

Do not follow where the path may lead. Go instead where there is no path and leave a trail. -Harold R. McAlindon

Everyone is looking for a role model. Usually our elders, teachers and learned doctors fit that bill. But as you already know, they don't hold all the answers. Exceptional role models may be difficult and sometimes impossible to find.

When it comes down to the bottom line, **YOU** are the leader that you have been looking for. Only **YOU** know the best solution for the challenges that lay on **YOUR** path. And with a little soul searching, and contemplating, **YOU** will usually choose the best options. There are no wrong choices. Only feedback. So if you do not get the outcome that you wanted, then you need to step back, reassess and then try a different way. The right result will eventually come, but only after a bit of trial and error. You mustn't give up so easily.

Usually, when there is no clear path, most of us will follow whoever speaks the loudest or whoever speaks with the most authority. Having a *sheeple* (people who behave as sheep) mentality and not thinking for yourself, will not get you to **YOUR** destination. It will keep you following the herd and being like everyone else. Even worse, you will usually end up being unnoticed in the herd, being pooped on by other sheeple, or stepping into other sheeple's poop.

Now is the time to step out from the masses and into your own spotlight of individuality. And don't look back. Believe in yourself and your innate greatness, and go from there. There are no mistakes, no errors. You are perfect starting from this point forward.

Close your eyes; take a deep breath and bask in that glow of **YOUR** uniqueness for a few minutes.

Now find a mirror, gaze deep into your own eyes and say, "I accept myself unconditionally, right now." Or look into your child's eyes and say, "I accept my beautiful child unconditionally, right now."

Do that two or three times every day, and watch how your entire life will shift. Feeling gratitude and showing love for yourself and your child, regardless of your situation will have a tremendous effect on each your future outcomes.

And by integrating some of our suggestions on a daily basis, you and your child will continue to get brighter, sharper and healthier. Inborn gifts will flourish and stressful sensitivities will diminish.

If your world is an overwhelming place, and you are in need of guidance, remember that you have the key that opens the door to your greatness. You may not know the right answer intellectually, but if you simply ask, let go of all expectations, and wait patiently to receive, the answer will come. There is an inherent synchronicity that flows through the universe. Allow it to flow into your life.

It is our hope that we, individually and collectively, step out of the matrix, speak *our* truth and see *our* world as it really is.

When we do what we need to do, learn what we need to learn, only then, we will become who we are meant to be.

Wake up and live our dreams. We are all one. As we treasure our own children, we inspire and enable others to do the same for theirs.

Be the *Enlightened Indigo Child* that you were born to be. It is your birthright.

It is your glory. Accept it.

NOTES
***

Made in the USA
Charleston, SC
09 July 2012